25
TO
LIFE

A Look at the Corrections
Department Through the Eyes
of an Officer of 25 Years

WAULEE EVANS

NEWMAN SPRINGS PUBLISHING
320 Broad Street
Red Bank, NJ 07701

First originally published by Newman Springs Publishing 2023

ISBN 978-1-68498-463-3 (Paperback)
ISBN 979-8-89308-620-1 (Hardcover)
ISBN 978-1-68498-464-0 (Digital)

Printed in the United States of America

ACKNOWLEDGMENTS

I was inspired to write this book to show my kids that whatever they want to do in life, they should go for it. My sons, Justin B. Evans and Branden H. Evans, and my daughters, Amelia E. Evans and Samantha Levy—y'all have always been my motivation. May God continue to guide you and bless you. Also, I would like to honor my sisters, Joann Evans and Brenda Evans, and my father, Walter Evans Sr. (gone but not forgotten). We love you all, and we are missing you!

These are the few people who definitely had a role in my journey in life: Melissa Evans and my Eighth Avenue family (Mount Vernon)—Eddie Brown, Ira Jackson, Harold Lucas, Butch Mack, Pop, Sissy Mims, Aunt Annie, Gator, Doc (Nolan), Darren Swanson, Gilbert Shearer, Tim Saxton, Roger Saxton, Dale Mims, Bernice Evans, Mark and Janet Jones, Uncle William Buggie, Uncle Luther, Aunt Pearl, Kenny Bongo, Tizz, Carlton Garrett, Walter Evans Sr., Ronald Hutchison, Arlett Lee, and Tyrone Evans—I just want to say thanks! Thanks to my niece and nephew, Monique L. Smith and Maurice Jones, for all their help. Nothing but love. I may have missed a few names. It's not personal. I'm getting old.

I'd like to thank my wife, Melissa, for always being there for our family when I had to work extra shifts and holidays. She held it down while still maintaining her career and keeping things moving smoothly in my absence. I'm blessed in many ways, but two of my biggest blessings have been my wife and the family we have created. I thank God since the day he connected us together and continues to bless our union and family.

INFORMATION PAGE

During the writing of this book, I was informed that in 2022, the governor of New York, Kathy Hochul, signed into law removing the word *inmate* when referring to people serving time in jail or prison. Now the correct term is *incarcerated person*. Prison reform advocates have said the term *inmate* has a dehumanizing effect, and prisoners feel it's degrading to be called an inmate. So throughout this book, you are going to read *incarcerated person* instead of *inmate* so I will be within the legal guidelines of New York State and up to date and politically correct with the term *incarcerated person*. I admit it will be something for a lot of people to get used to, but I agree with the change, and it does sound somewhat better than the previous word the Department of Corrections and other agencies were using.

INTRODUCTION

I remember a few years before I even thought about working for the Department of Corrections, a few correction offi- cers came to our playground in Mount Vernon on Eighth Avenue for recruitment purposes, and I was the main per- son saying nobody wants to be a paid prisoner, nobody wants to work in a jail, and it's almost comical that five years later I took the job. I had a friend who took the test with me, and he had the interview around the same time, but when it was time to go into the academy, he took a dif- ferent job offer. I don't really regret taking the job because everything I ever went through in life prepared me for the day I walked into that building. It's a dog-eat-dog world in jail, and sometimes the people you least expect will try to cause you the most problems. It's an environment where you can never let your guard down because that's when you will take the hardest hit. Maybe not physically, but you have to protect yourself every second you are in that place. I say this throughout the book: my motto in jail is don't trust anybody. Working in a jail is unlike working anywhere else in the world. Along with your training, you also need an abundance of common sense and a certain level of street smarts. Without those important attributes, you are either going to have a long, horrible career, or you just won't make it to the finish line (retirement).

Also, an open mind is a must. Most things are not what they appear to the naked eye. Although experience will be your best teacher, staying alert will be your best asset. Stay aware of your surroundings and remember no one person has all the answers. I don't care what their job title is; again, this is totally my perspective on how I visualize the Department of Corrections and its environment. While I was there, I met some really good people in my twenty-five-year career—officers and incarcerated persons. I also ran into a few individuals I could have definitely done without. Overall, my career was somewhat normal, nothing outrageous or outlandish where a jail is concerned. The majority of corrections officers are decent, hardworking people trying to make a living and feed their families. However, there are some officers determined to do their own thing, and they are the ones you read about. There were times when I felt more comfortable around the incarcerated persons than I did with some of the officers. And I'm sure if you took a poll, many more officers than myself would say the same thing. Jail consists of multiple personalities on both sides.

If you come into jail with some loud, boisterous nonsense, whether you're an officer or an incarcerated person, you're going to get attention you really don't want. And being that it's a jail, you can quickly paint yourself into a corner. I have seen all types of people paint themselves into a corner, from the incarcerated persons to the officers. We even had a supervisor who thought it couldn't happen to him, and the next thing he knew, he was airborne, body-slammed, and off to the hospital in an ambulance. Basically, if you're trying to be something you're not, you're going to get exposed—it's just a matter of time. It's just that simple. I can't stress it enough: be yourself, because pretending to be someone you're not could be bad for your health. Real recognize real, and real recognize fake too! There is definitely no future in fronting—meaning pretending you're something you are not isn't going to work.

I have many different views of the correctional system, as an officer, as a civilian, as a parent, and as a human being. I had some friends unfortunately in the system, and relatives going to jail, and having worked in the jail for over twenty-five years, you get to understand both sides of the system. People go to jail for many different reasons and circumstances. No judgment—life is about choices, and things happen in life where you only have a split second to make a choice that can affect your entire life moving forward. Anybody can go to jail; it doesn't automatically make you a bad person. Just like putting on a correctional officer's uniform doesn't automatically make you a good person.

History has shown me throughout my career that integrity isn't exclusive to a certain type of person or any occupation. You can look the part but still not be living the part; that's why people say action speaks louder than words. We had officers who were held hostage by the incarcerated persons. It's a horrible situation, I imagine, to be in, no matter what side you find yourself on. And there are no guarantees you're going to come out of that situation the same way you went in. You had officers running out of the building or risking being taken hostage. Safety and security are of major importance in jail at all times. But at any time, a jail can go left for a number of reasons, which makes the job extremely dangerous, and you never know when you're about to have the worst day in your career or your life. You have to stay alert and aware of your surroundings—nobody can do it for you. Being a hostage, I imagine, can be a traumatic experience for all officers and staff involved.

Some incarcerated persons are always looking for ways to get out of jail early (escape). We had an incarcerated person who hid in the garbage and was taken outside through the kitchen. We also had an incarcerated person who climbed the fence in the rec yard with everybody in the yard having recreation and officers in the yard. I still can't believe it, but that's how fast things can happen in jail. That's why I can't stress the importance of being alert because you never know when you are going to be involved in the same kind of situation like those officers not seeing the incarcerated person climbing the fence.

Twenty-five years of my life went into this job. That's a long commitment to something that's unpredictable, chaotic, dangerous, and toxic as a jail and penitentiary. I have tried to write about some incidents and situations that I can't forget and remember a few details of how it went down. I think every year I worked there, somebody was getting fired for something. I don't have enough information to say whether I think the department was justified in letting some of them go. But certainly, we all have our opinions.

I remember in the penitentiary there was a fire in the blocks almost every week from the incarcerated persons setting their mattress on fire and smoking up the whole block. I never could understand how you set a fire in a cell that you are locked in?

Years ago, corrections changed the mattresses to a new flame-resistant material, and the fires in the blocks are no longer a situation officers have to deal with. The majority of the new officers never had to deal with fires their whole career thus far. The jail has changed over the years, some good, some bad, but overall the officers make it work.

When I first started the job, I knew several officers who were already working there, but the only officers from Mount Vernon that showed me any type of hometown courtesy and Mount Vernon love were these four officers: Sissy Mims, Denise Andrews, James Bess, and Leonard Perry. These officers looked out from day one. If there was something I needed, information, assistance, they came through. I have the utmost respect for my brothers and sisters from Mount Vernon. Two of them have gone on to be with the Lord, and I pray God has received them with open arms because they were definitely heaven-sent. And as for Mims and Bess, I will never forget the love you guys showed from day one. You already know, friends until the end.

CHAPTER 1

My name is Walter Evans, and most people called me Waulee Wobs growing up. I grew up in a small town in Westchester County called Mount Vernon, New York. Back in the day, our town was known for basketball until Heavy D. and the Boyz put us on the map with rap. It's a small town, four square miles, and everybody knew each other back in the day, and the young had respect for the old, and everybody stayed in their lane. It was nothing like it is now—people appear to be getting shot on a regular basis. That's totally unacceptable, and something has to be done. There appears to be no rules or respect in the street, just reckless gunplay and innocent people being killed. It's definitely a shame.

Growing up, people used to refer to Mount Vernon as "Money Earning Mount Vernon," but over the years, with the increase in homicides, I hear people now refer to Mount Vernon as "Murderville"—definitely not a name the residents of Mount Vernon can be proud of, I'm sure.

I have lost cousins, friends, and associates to the streets of Mount Vernon. A lot of good people have been killed in the streets of Mount Vernon. I grew up in those same streets, but I'm optimistic that things will get better, and the town will return to the nice place to live that it used to be. Although Mount Vernon has changed drastically over the years, most of the stores we used to shop at on Fourth Avenue are no longer there; they probably relocated to another town or went out of business. Brush Park, Memorial Field, Fourth Street Playground, and Eighth Avenue Playgrounds were some of our hangout spots. Also the Boys Club on Sixth Avenue. There was always a lot to do in Mount Vernon. On a recent visit, I noticed the YMCA on Second Avenue had closed down. I have a lot of good memories growing up in Mount Vernon. It was nothing like you see on the news now.

I am hopeful that the people in Mount Vernon get it together and turn the city away from where it's headed because it was a great place to live back in the day. However, Mount Vernon took a drastic hit in the mid-80s. The whole country was blindsided by a new drug called crack. It was spreading throughout the world like a forest fire and just as difficult to put out. Unfortunately, Mount Vernon was one of the many cities in Westchester that was devastated by the surge of this new drug, crack cocaine. People were being arrested in record numbers, and the jail was filling up with limited space. With the jail population increasing, it created a multitude of jobs in law enforcement, especially in the Department of Corrections. I remember my first time in a correctional facility; I went to visit a friend of mine who was in prison in upstate New York.

I remember it was really busy. A lot was going on in the visiting room, and they had many vending machines where you could get a soda and a sandwich. It really didn't feel like a jail visiting room. I can't really explain the vibe, but it wasn't anything close to what I had imagined it to be. I left that jail that day, saying to myself, *I could do that job.* And in 1988, I began working in the penitentiary in Valhalla, Westchester County, New York. At this time, the crack epidemic was at its peak. The jail was crowded beyond anything anyone had ever seen before. We were running out of space to put the incarcerated persons, and we started turning basic closets into cells to accommodate the influx of incarcerated persons arriving at the jail. Temporary housing was made called M unit. It was like a shelter on steroids. M unit was a giant room filled with what looked like a sea of metal bunk beds.

M unit consisted of approximately seventy incarcerated persons and two officers. The place was dirty, hot, and humid, and nothing less than mass confusion. You were constantly on your feet the whole shift because something was always going on, and as an officer, it's your job to make sure nobody gets hurt or violated on your watch. Due to the overcrowding and the shortage of staff, new officers were coming into the building with only two weeks of training. We were thrown into a situation where a lot of officers were not ready for that environment. It was so uncomfortably hot in M unit, with the large floor fans blowing hot air all over the place. We were allowed to work in T-shirts. However, the lack of training caught a lot of the officers off guard. Some officers were getting robbed in the blocks and assaulted and not reporting it. Some were also getting extorted in the blocks. Officers were quitting and walking right off their post and out the building.

When I first started working in the pen, it was a madhouse. Some of the officers never reported that they were being extorted or robbed because they were either scared or embarrassed, or both. I saw officers walking out of the building crying. Now that I was thinking about it, that was crazy. The job is not for everybody, especially back then when there were no body alarms, no cameras, not even a whistle. And some officers became overwhelmed by the environment. The job is more mental than physical. If you're easily intimidated, the job is probably not for you. An officer was quitting every week when I first started. A few officers were locked in closets and cells. Some had their cigarettes taken from them by the incarcerated persons. I wouldn't have believed it if I hadn't heard some of them talking about what had happened to them to other officers. It's the type of job where you have to be observant to see who is who because when I first started, some officers were worse than some of the incarcerated persons, and that's a fact. It's already a dangerous environment, then add these unreliable officers to the mix, now you're playing with fire and you're closer to hell than you realize. Now you are working in a very dangerous situation because your help is really hurting you, no matter what profession you're in. There are always a few that dance out of step if you know what I mean, and there's definitely no shame in their game. So in corrections, it's a good idea to look before you leap because you could step in something you can't easily wipe off your feet (a little humor, relax).

When you take over a block, you usually receive several keys from the previous officer because the keys are old and worn, and the numbers are not legible. Every officer has their own method of how they know what key is what. Some officers use colored rubber bands or different color strings. Knowing your keys could mean how long it's going to take for you to open your doors in case of an emergency. Not knowing your keys in an emergency can make five minutes feel like an hour. Back in the day, we didn't have ERT. It was all available officers running to the code. I feel like the officers were closer back then; we had cook-outs and Christmas parties and a softball team. All of those events over the years went the way of the dinosaur. They don't exist now. Your partner is a very important person in jail. That's why it helps to know who you're working with because if you find out during a problem, it's probably too late, and I don't like surprises. We had an officer run out of the block with his partner wrestling on the floor with two incarcerated persons. He ran out of the block looking for help when he was supposed to be the help. We had another officer who took a beating while his partner watched because the incarcerated persons told him, "Don't move, stay right there, or you get a beat down too." I didn't know the officer that well, but I had to ask him if it was true what I'm hearing. He said, "Yeah, I was scared." I never worked with him ever after he told me that. To help, all you have to do is knock the phone off the hook, and then help is coming. Nobody says you have to be Superman in there, but you can't always be Clark Kent.

Departments of Correction is a job; you have to know who you are, or the incarcerated persons are going to tell you who you are going to be. A jail can be calm one minute and the next, all hell can break loose. All it takes is one person to set it off and get things going; it's like lighting a match to gasoline. You can't let that fire spread to anything or anyone else. I titled this book *25 to Life* because as a corrections officer, we give this job twenty-five years of our lives; and unfortunately, most officers give this job their lives before they reach twenty-five years. Being in a jail environment is just as stressful for the officer as it is for the incarcerated persons. This book will show the similarities between the incarcerated persons and the corrections officer and the effects that jail has on both of our lives.

After being in that environment for twenty years or more, how can anyone come out of that and not have some form of PTSD (post-traumatic stress disorder)? It's almost impossible. Being exposed to jail can definitely have a negative effect on a person. It amazes me how we are basically doing time side by side with the incarcerated person, and we think it doesn't affect us. It's like standing in the rain when you both get wet, and don't you both feel the same effects of the rain? Well, jail is the same way; we are both exposed to the same environment and almost treated the same in a lot of ways. We both do time side by side, for the officer and the inmates. The first time we enter the jail, we both probably feel a certain level of anxiety because of the unknown, because if nothing else, a jail is unpredictable. You anticipate the worst because it's jail, and everything you've heard about jail up to this point hasn't been good.

So you approach this endeavor cautiously and alert. But above all, you must be yourself because if you try being something you're not, the incarcerated person will see right through that, and things will go downhill from there. According to statistics, the average life expectancy of a corrections officer is fifty-eight years or five years after retirement. With those odds, we would have to be crazy not to try and change up a few things so we can spend more time on earth with our families. A study was conducted, and it was determined that every two years spent in jail takes one year off your life. Not really much to look forward to if those numbers are accurate. We have to do better, especially when we know better, period. Incarcerated persons also die at a higher rate and much younger age than most officers, so none of us are really in a position to point fingers or celebrate.

We're both on this sinking ship together. As corrections officers, we sacrifice a lot of our quality time, most of our adult lives, and our health (physically and mentally) just to maintain a job. Year after year, we continue to lose good officers and productive people in the jail community to an abundance of heart attacks, strokes, suicides, alcohol abuse, and illegal drug consumption. It's happening so frequently that the majority of officers think it's a normal part of life. Death is a natural part of life, but not on the frequent scale corrections officers find themselves. Going to a memorial service or funeral every other month is not normal. What is that building doing to officers, or they're losing their lives and, on occasion, their minds? This stuff is not normal, but nobody seems interested in getting to the bottom of this.

What's being done or can be done to try and reduce or eliminate the silent assassins that are wreaking havoc on the lives of the corrections officers and their families? It's not normal or acceptable to continue to watch the demise of so many officers who succumb to the hazardous environment of the jail, and it appears nothing is being done about it to at least attempt to prevent this atrocious dilemma from happening. It's borderline inhumane as far as I'm concerned. One of the enticing things about the job was the overtime;

most officers double their salaries, but at what cost? What price do we pay trying to get paid? I was told early in my career overtime was blood money. Now I see what they were talking about, especially when you see where all the overtime kings and queens are now; it's beyond sad when you think about it.

When you work too much, you become exhausted mentally and physically, and your alertness is almost nonexistent. Not a good look when you're being paid to be observant. I look back over my career, and we all did overtime, some more than others. And we had forced overtime, where you were forced to work an extra shift. You had some officers who always went to the emergency room when they got forced to work an extra shift; they did it on a regular basis every time they were forced to work. And when they make sergeant now, they have amnesia and don't remember when they used to go to the emergency room. But what's really crazy is now they are the ones calling up officers, forcing them to work, and have the nerve to say these officers don't want to work. It's unbelievable; you can't make this up.

Life as we know it can change in the blink of an eye. In a matter of seconds, with no warning, your whole life can become upside down. That's why you need to be alert at all times. We had an officer who was talking with an irate incarcerated person, and the officer had his hands in his pockets. The discussion escalated into an argument, and the incarcerated person broke the officer's jaw. How do you protect yourself if your hands are in your pockets? Any given day, you can walk around the pen and the jail and see officers walking around with their hands in their pockets, and nobody ever says anything about it. I'm sure the incarcerated persons notice it too. To me, it's just someone showing that they don't understand their surroundings. Officers get written up for wearing a wrong-colored T-shirt but are not written up for having both hands stuffed in their pockets. Please, can somebody make this make sense? What's more of a security concern?

That officer could have lost his life if he would have hit his head the wrong way. Needless to say, his career is over. Just before I retired, this officer was working at one center controlling the gates. Supposedly, the officer and an incarcerated person got into a disagreement, and the incarcerated person pitched a shutout. The officer came to the clinic. I didn't recognize him as his head was swollen. In my twenty-five years working there, I had never seen anything like that. Now he is a supervisor; you can't make this up. One thing I learned working in the jail is that if you give an incarcerated person respect, they most of the time will give you respect. Nobody really wants drama at the end of the day. It's unbelievable what you can observe in jail on a daily basis. Some officers don't realize incarcerated persons are grown men and women too, just like the officers. They are not your kids, so don't talk to them like they are. That should be Corrections 101.

We had a few women officers that I would rather work with than some of the men. Don't get me wrong; most of the officers had no problem doing the job, but working with some officers meant you were in for a long day. As I write this book, these are the incidents I remember the most. I know the climate of the jail has changed; incarcerated persons sexually harassing the female officers is on the rise. Nobody's mother, grandmother, wife, or daughter comes to work expecting to be constantly disrespected day after day. That just goes to show me how things change because I remember there was a time when an incarcerated person wouldn't let another incarcerated person verbally disrespect a female officer. It just goes to show the times we are living in now. However, it's a problem that needs to be dealt with now before it gets worse. Today it's verbal; no telling where it can go from here, so legally let's nip this in the bud now.

We are already dealing with a life expectancy deficit, and some officers don't make it any better. Every officer's goal should be to go home at the end of the day the same way they came in: uninjured and healthy. But only if we could live in a perfect world, which we don't, and the rest is history in jail. Both the officer and the incarcerated person have to make a few adjustments to coexist in jail life. The only difference I see is that when the incarcerated person has difficulty adjusting to jail life, they go into protective custody. When an officer has difficulty adjusting to jail life, he either quits or gets fired. Again, I can't say this enough: the job is not for everybody, just like a life of crime is not really for anybody. There are better ways to make a living than the illegal route. Increase your education, and you increase your options. However, we have officers who are the equivalent of being in protective custody. They can't work around your average incarcerated person, so they are at the supervisor's mercy and will do anything to stay out of the blocks, and I do mean anything. Where do they find these people?

I can't stress it enough: the job isn't for everybody, and again it's more mental than physical, but you should still try to be in the best possible shape you can be for health reasons. I remember before ERT, it was everybody available who responded to codes, and we had officers who didn't even bother running to codes because they knew they weren't going to make it there, and if they did make it there, they had nothing left to break up an altercation, so why bother? ERT saved a lot of officers' lives just from the fact that the officer no longer has to respond to the codes. That makes a big difference. Officers have always been injured on the job with all the steel and concrete. I'm surprised the numbers of injured officers haven't gone through the roof. My hand got slammed in the mailbox in control once—the worst pain I have ever felt in my hands in life. It was an accident, but it still hurt like crazy. I could have lost a finger or two, but thank God I didn't.

Your appearance should command just as much respect as your presence does. Looking neat and sharp; however, there is always one or two who look like they slept in their clothes before coming to work. How is somebody going to respect that? We had an officer who used to wear pajama slippers with his uniform. How professional is it that he wore those slippers on his post while doing his job? Imagine wearing slippers on a concrete floor; that's like the equivalent of wearing roller skates. How serious do you think the incarcerated persons are going to take this person? When he was miraculously promoted to sergeant, nobody took him seriously because of how unprofessional he was as an officer. He was a lousy officer, so you knew he was going to be a lousy supervisor. So that brings me back to my point. In most professions, no matter what you do for a living, your appearance is a big part of your job. Think about it, would you let a lawyer represent you wearing shorts and a tank top? I don't think so, and that would definitely not go over well with the judge as well. There's a saying, "Don't dress for the job you have, dress for the job you want"— meaning keep your appearance together regardless.

Both the officer and the incarcerated persons are away from their families for long periods of time. The officer who does sixteen hours a day is the equivalent of the incarcerated person's doing twenty-four hours a day because the officer has to travel home, shower, sleep, and return within the remaining eight hours left. Returning home at night around eleven thirty isn't quality time to spend with your family but just to eat and sleep. As an officer, that puts a strain on most relationships because you're at work when the family needs you the most, not when they're sleeping. Law enforcement hours can be anytime of the day because the jail never closes. I don't know any officers whose marriages and relationships haven't been affected because of the hours worked at the jail. I'm almost certain overtime is the culprit of many divorces taking place through the Department of Corrections. However, I don't think it's totally the sole culprit of all divorces officers are going through. But it does play a part.

The job is very hard on relationships and marriages because you're always at work, and when you're home, more than likely, you're sleeping, trying to get some rest to prepare for another day. The Department of Corrections is not the ideal place to work if you're trying to establish some kind of bond with your significant other because you don't have the time; you're usually preoccupied with work or sleep. And when an officer has had a drama-filled day, the last thing they need is to come home to more drama; you need peace, and no substitute will do.

I have seen officers go through some horrible changes and moments because their personal lives and relationships started to unravel. You never know what a person is going through, and that goes for the incarcerated person as well. You have to be alert enough to know if there is a change in someone's behavior. Do they appear depressed? Picking up on something as simple as that could save a life. Suicide is a serious issue that has affected officers and incarcerated persons throughout my whole career. It has to be one of the worst situations anyone has to deal with on either side, be it a corrections officer or incarcerated person.

Depression is real, and being overwhelmed by depression is a dangerous place to be, but no situation in life is bad enough that you take your own life. I pray to anybody who is reading this, if you or someone you know feels depressed and doesn't feel like you can talk to someone about your problems, please talk to somebody. Call the suicide and crisis lifeline at #988 because your life is worth saving. Nobody should feel like their life doesn't matter. You may not see it, but everyone's life matters. This is personal to me because I spoke to an officer who took his life approximately thirty minutes after I spoke to him. I had no clue; he was smiling like everything was okay. I will never forget that. God bless anybody who is going through something right now and feels overwhelmed. This too shall pass. If God brings you to it, he will bring you through it. Just have faith. You already won the victory.

One thing about a jail: something is always going on inside. No two days are exactly alike. One question I have never asked an incarcerated person was, "What does it feel like being locked up and doing time?" However, a few volunteered to give the information and said, "It's a form of torture." You see your loved ones on a visit, but you can't go home with them. You get letters and pictures of missed kids' birthday parties and graduations. You miss out on so much that your role at home almost gets diminished, and there is nothing you can do about it. Overall, you miss quality time with your family, and to add to that, a jail is one of the most toxic environments you can find yourself in.

The jail's structure goes against nature. Imagine trying to keep a deer in captivity in a four-by-four cubicle. It would appear to go crazy and become destructive because it's not their natural habitat.

Sometimes you have to ask yourself, Is the reason why so many officers and incarcerated persons struggle in the jail environment because it's not our natural habitat? We are used to being free and smelling what's left of the fresh air, feeling the warm sun on our skin, and not being restricted to a cubicle with recycled air recirculating throughout the building. I can't help but make the connection to an unhealthy environment that adds up to sick officers and incarcerated persons who are stressed out. It's an unnatural environment, to say the least. Just imagine living in your own bathroom for six months or a year straight. Most of us would go crazy. I think just as many officers deal with depression as incarcerated persons, but it's not something you're going to get the average officer to talk about.

Writing this book was somewhat therapeutic for me because it's like taking twenty-five years of this morbid environment and exhaling twenty-five years of being exposed to a continuous display of negativity that will affect anyone. I salute the veteran officers who came long before us because there is no doubt in my mind that as hard as the jail was or is on us, I'm sure without a shadow of a doubt that the pioneers of the Department of Corrections had to have it way worse than officers have it at present. Until we figure out why so many officers get sick, have heart attacks, strokes, and a host of other illnesses, we have way more work to do outside the blocks than we do inside the blocks - finding answers to some of our questions. We shouldn't have to receive the equivalent of a life sentence because we signed up for a job that requires us to do twenty-five years in one of the most horrible conditions one can imagine in the Department of Corrections; mentally, it's torture. It was somewhat cleaner before I retired, but the vibe is a downer. Too many people pretending to know when they really don't know anything, and their suggestions and their faulty decision-making are getting people hurt.

Mental illness plays a major role in the Department of Corrections, especially since a governor called for the closing of all unnecessary beds in psychiatric centers, better known as mental institutions, in New York. Those patients didn't just disappear but walk aimlessly throughout New York, with some being arrested and getting caught up in the correctional system. In my years working in the system, I truly believe that not only do the incarcerated persons fall through the cracks of the mental illness system, but it also filters down into society, where this problem is becoming society's problem. I have seen several videos where an individual goes into a liquor store and breaks every bottle in there, or a person goes on a subway platform and pushes somebody in front of a moving train, or a person goes into a restaurant and fights everybody that's in there. Every one of these people, in their defense, the lawyer said they forgot to take their meds. So in all likelihood, at some point, they will be back on the street causing more chaos because New York taxpayers are no longer footing their bill in a psychiatric facility. So I guess random people and businesses will continue to be under attack, and insurance companies continue to pay for these out-of-control psychiatric outbursts. Problem solved? Not even close.

Don't get me wrong; I'm not trying to be insensitive to the mental illness community. I'm just saying it's doing them and society a disservice to close down so many facilities and help centers that cater to their medical and physical well-being. Unfortunately, more and more people with mental illnesses are finding themselves in the Department of Corrections because of their limited options and their behavior from being off their meds for long periods of time. And the shelters are already too dangerous for the average person seeking shelter, let alone one who also has mental issues. A shelter probably wouldn't be a good choice for someone dealing with a mental illness; it would only add to the problem and not contribute to a solution. So I guess until this issue is given the attention it needs and deserves, we will continue to see and hear about people with mental illnesses being charged with crimes they have no memory or understanding of.

Most jails nowadays have a facility where they house and treat incarcerated persons whom they suspect may have a mental issue. It's also the most dangerous part of the jail you can work in; more officers get injured on that post than any post in the jail, and nothing ever changes, just the name of the officer that works there. As a corrections officer, you get all types of incarcerated persons on your block; however, an incarcerated person experiencing some type of mental illness episode can turn your peaceful block into a complete nightmare. Years ago, we had an incarcerated person who swallowed anything he could get his hands on: coins, pencils, pens, glass, plastic, watches—you name it, he swallowed it. The hospitals had to go into his stomach so often they made a zipper on his stomach. We had another incarcerated person who was into self-mutilation. He probably cut himself every day; he would make knives out of anything—his eating utensils, a pencil, a pen, anything he could get his hands on. Again these individuals were into hurting themselves, but every once in a while, they would attack the officer for whatever reason. And to think, at some point, this person will be back on the street in society. But I think the real concern is that for every mental patient we have in the Department of Corrections, there are hundreds more walking the streets of New York and beyond. That's why I can't stress the importance of being alert at all times. I understand how in some situations it was just a matter of seconds (not much of a warning), but just being observant to your surroundings will cut down on a lot of nonsense you have to deal with.

I admit there is a difference between being mentally ill and reckless. But normally, when we see or hear about an officer acting reckless, we may also be quick to label them a mental patient as well. I remember when I was working in the pen, there were two officers living in the men's locker room, and from what I was told, they were told several times they couldn't live in there; they turned the showers into a bedroom for both of them. Some would try to argue the point that these officers were mentally ill. One of them also didn't own a car—not implying no car ownership is an indication of mental illness, but someone needing a ride to work every day can be considered a red flag. Both of them were eventually fired, but the most important question is how did they get hired in the first place?

We had an officer who was shooting cans with his off-duty weapon in a public park; that would fall under recklessness, but a strong argument could be made for mental illness as well because who in their right mind would do that? We also had an officer who got into an altercation with somebody on the street and pulled his off-duty weapon out and shot into the air—what he said were warning shots. When they do that, a warning shot, what goes up must come down. Reckless or mental illness? That's a close one. All these officers have one thing in common: they were fired. I wasn't friends with any of these officers that were fired, but I'm just trying to show the reader of this book that just like an incarcerated person can turn their life around and live a productive and progressive life, an officer can throw it all away just as quickly as one, two, three. It's not about labels and titles; it's about who you are as a human being and who you are as a person. It's just as easy to do the right thing as it is to do the wrong thing, but most of us just sometimes pick the hard way of doing things.

When we hear the word *institutionalized*, normally, we think the term is reserved for the incarcerated person exclusively, meaning they have been incarcerated so long they have nothing but jail habits. But in my twenty-five-year career, the word *institutionalized* can describe an officer as well. I observed that within my first thirty days on the job. I saw what looked like officers in their seventies slap-boxing with the incarcerated persons, and you could see the officers lost their natural reflexes at least twenty-five years ago; plus they were using slang that seemed to have played out ten years ago (at least), and they were bopping up and down the halls like they were in their early twenties (even the word *bopping* means something else now; in my day, *bopping* means walking). Looking back on that scene, it looks so crazy to me, and I was saying to myself, *I hope that's not me when I'm about to retire.*

A lot of these officers seemed like late bloomers who were trying to relive their high school days. You couldn't help but laugh. I actually witnessed officers trying to get street credibility from the incarcerated persons. It's a different world inside the jail; it's like living in a place that time forgot. However, the incarcerated person is very creative and resourceful. The majority of them make the best out of a bad situation. That's where I think the similarities change between the officers and the incarcerated persons. The incarcerated person, in my estimation, seems more comfortable in the jail situation than the average officer. I think that the officer is more stressed out in the jail environment than the incarcerated persons because of the unattainable expectations the officer has of jail, the noise level, being outnumbered in the pods—the ratio is sixty inmates to one officer—that can be a distraction for an officer because it doesn't take a genius to know the numbers are not in the officer's favor. Sometimes in jail, when you think from a logical perspective, you put yourself in an awkward position because most of your dealings in jail are from an illogical perspective. It's like you're trying to think rationally when the situations mostly consist of a person being irrational.

When you learn to balance that out, then it will start to make more sense to you. It's a major mental adjustment, believe me. Another element that threatens the safety and security of the jail is contraband. For those of you who are not familiar with the term *contraband*, it is anything in the jail an incarcerated person is not allowed to have; for instance, cigarettes, illegal drugs, alcohol, weed, and the list goes on. This is by far one of the worst dilemmas the jail has to deal with. The jail, for the most part, does a good job in checking for contraband, but no system is perfect, especially when employees are part of the problem. Mostly, every occupation in the jail has been caught trying to bring contraband into the building. Nurses, teachers, maintenance workers, and even officers have been caught trying to bring in contraband to the jail.

When you think about it, why would a person risk their job and freedom bringing in anything into the building unless they were scared, being extorted, or just flat out being manipulated by the incarcerated person? A scared employee in a jail environment is a security breach and a major liability because it endangers everyone else trying to do their job. Drugs continue to be a problem inside the jails today, and the drugs they are using now not only get these individuals high, but they're killing them. The overdose rate has almost tripled since opioids and fentanyl have entered the picture of drug use, and it's wreaking havoc on the illegal drug-using community. More people are dying from illegal drug use than gun violence in the United States.

Something has to be done to stop this epidemic because, believe it or not, we all are affected by this situation one way or another.

Weapons are a major problem in jail; the homemade knives are the weapon of choice in jail. These weapons are manufactured in the blocks with whatever incarcerated person can get their hands on; they can make a weapon out of almost anything. When I was working there, we were supposed to get stab vests, but it never happened. I hope they have them now because they are very much needed. I hope they don't wait until something happens to an officer to get them.

Drugs sometimes come through the visiting room, where the incarcerated person usually attempts to swallow a balloon with drugs. However, the jail has a system where when they suspect an incarcerated person of ingesting a controlled substance, they are taken to the infirmary, handcuffed to the bed, and given a bedpan to defecate in. The officer is supposed to go through the person's feces looking for drugs. I always refused that detail every time I was assigned to that post. I refused to do it because it's degrading to ask somebody to do that; plus it's not something we learned in the academy. So why ask an officer to do it? They tried to get the nursing staff to do it, but they refused also. So now they get the officer who will do anything and question nothing. I can't see how they think that's okay to get someone to go through someone else's feces with a wooden stick.

It's demoralizing to ask a person to do that. Just to say no, you were not taught that in the academy, and they are assuming you know what drugs look like because you were never shown. That is very interesting. I don't think the average person knows how dangerous the inside of a jail is. I hear people saying all the time that when a family member is locked up, at least they don't have to worry about them, and you know where they are. That's false; almost anything can happen to an incarcerated person in jail that can happen to them in the streets. I know most people's perception of jail is what they see on TV or based on something someone told them that's been to jail and distorted the truth. Homemade knives are plentiful in jail, and the inmates who don't have one know how to make one.

In jail, just like on the streets, you don't need an argument to lead up to something; no words have to ever be exchanged. Just simply looking in the direction of someone looking for trouble, and then it's on.

Another thing that is a sign of the times: this new young generation appears not to respect anything; everything is confrontational with them. The number of assaults on officers is constantly on the rise. Women officers, in particular, have been involved in more physical assaults and verbal sexual assaults over the last few years as well. Just before I retired, I noticed they were installing cameras throughout the buildings. Cameras can help you or hurt you depending on who is viewing them. And some officers are going to be reluctant to get involved in incidents because of the Monday morning quarterback syndrome that will definitely be taking place.

You more than likely will be second-guessed, or someone is going to say you should have done this or you should have done that. Nobody should be scrutinized when you're trying to save your life or somebody else's life. The cameras represent someone always looking over your shoulder, and it's easy to say what you would have done in a certain situation, but unless you're actually in that situation, it's speculation and not facts. The stress in jail seems to affect the officer and the incarcerated person. That toxic environment of negativity is like an invisible plague that has consumed the jail, and the collateral damage is the officers and the incarcerated persons. However, for the jail to operate smoothly, it will take cooperation from the incarcerated persons and extreme professionalism from the officers.

One thing about the effects of stress on the body is you can't smell it, see it, or even touch it, but you better believe it's there. Aside from the chaos, confusion, and constant pandemonium you have to deal with in jail on a daily basis, there's drama around every corner. All eyes are on you from the cameras that cover almost every inch of the jail. On any given day, you can walk throughout the jail and see an abundance of disgruntled corrections officers, justifiably so, and someone on the receiving end of some disrespect. The jail is like playing chess and using real people as pawns. One mistake can have severe consequences, whether it was intentional or not. Jail is almost exactly like a microcosm of real life. Almost every outside-the-wall issue is dealt with inside the jail. I know that the motto "Trust no one" can appear a bit harsh, and hopefully you can find someone to trust on the job, but one thing is certain: it won't be easy.

People will fold on you quickly on that job. I don't want to write too much about the negativity of the jail, but if I look back over my career and pick out the five most horrible things that have happened to an officer, another officer had a lot to do with it. I'm going to leave that right there.

Just don't change who you are because then you're going to be totally lost. Let me get back on track. It's mind-boggling that we have so much information, and studies have been done, and nobody is taking that information and attempting to save officers' lives in the Department of Corrections. All across the country, there are suicides, strokes, and heart attacks killing officers year after year, and nothing is being done about it. The environment alone is stressful enough; just being in the jail can be overwhelming at times for both the officer and the incarcerated person. Compounded with problems in one's personal life, it definitely is a recipe for disaster.

We need to do more to preserve the quality of life for all people who work for the Department of Corrections. This is not a local problem; this is a problem that extends to all correctional facilities around the country. I guess we will continue going to funerals and memorial services until very few of us are left because it appears nothing is being done to improve the mental health and physical well-being of the officers. I guess we will continue to witness this Department of Corrections massacre that's taken place right before our eyes and convince everybody that it's just part of the job. All over the country, correctional officers are dying from all the same illnesses: strokes, heart attacks, suicides. What's really going on here?

Something as simple as having a dietitian in the jail approving the meals being offered to the officers and the incarcerated persons would be a major improvement and a step in the right direction. It's a start. Actually getting a healthy diet implemented would be a major accomplishment. Then maybe an exercise program; we have a lot of officers that know their way around the gym. I'm not talking about the ones that work out five days a week and still get chased out of the blocks. Y'all know who I'm talking about. Anyway, we all have to coexist in these blocks; what an incarcerated person is exposed to in the blocks, we officers are exposed to the same thing. I remember it used to be freezing on the blocks because the windows were knocked out in the summer to let air into the cells, and in the winter, it would be freezing. However, most of the incarcerated persons would be under those thick state blankets, and we would be freezing to death trying to make our rounds. I remember many nights like that.

I was somewhat relieved when I went to the day shift, but it was short-lived because I traded one problem for another. No matter what shift you work, you're going to be faced with some type of dilemma. Every day, it's something different, and no two days are identical; no days in jail are uneventful— one of the several buildings has some drama. As an officer, you can almost feel things when they are about to go left, and you have to be proactive before you're in the middle of some nonsense. You have some officers who avoid the blocks like it's a plague, and they have more war stories than a five-star general. I think the hardest part of being a corrections officer from my perspective is listening to somebody telling war stories, and you know they are not about that life.

Now the person is a know-it-all. It's frustrating and borderline demoralizing. If you took a survey in the jail, you would be surprised at how many officers have legitimate complaints about what they are forced to deal with on a daily basis. But nobody wants to rock the boat or get unwanted attention for speaking up and telling the truth, so the officers suffer in silence. Just like the incarcerated persons, they go against the grain, they are labeled a troublemaker or worse, so you see how we're all in the same boat. Don't let nobody try to convince you any differently. These are just a few examples of what it's like being a corrections officer in this jail environment. I thought the Department of Corrections was a civil service job, but they run it like a mom-and-pop deli.

Being a corrections officer is a thankless job; you're damned if you do and damned if you don't. There is no happy medium. Some officers like to work the control bubble because there is zero incarcerated person contact, but in my estimation, working in control is super boring, especially working with someone who could be equally boring—that's torture for a person like me. I like to talk to people, and it makes the time go quicker, and you learn what the vibe is in the building. The unpredictable aspects of the jail place an added stress on the officer and the incarcerated persons. The speculation is a killer in the jail. The officer speculating: Is he going to get forced to work overtime or placed on the minor block that's about to go left any minute? For the incarcerated person: What is the court going to say? How is the family surviving without them?

I know some people refer to Valhalla Jail as a country club compared to other jails in Upstate New York, but it's not a country club for everybody—just like some of the toughest jails in New York are not tough for everybody; somebody has it good in there, or the place wouldn't exist—it's probably a nightmare for most. In jail, a lot is riding on who you are as a person; usually, it determines what kind of experience you're going to have. Some people are not going to have a problem because of the way they carry themselves, and some people are going to invite all types of problems to themselves because of the way they carry themselves, if you know what I mean. Believe it or not, respect plays a big part in surviving in jail; you can't survive without it.

The incarcerated person has a lot to contend with being locked up. Your original time and sentence could double just by being in the wrong place at the wrong time. And let's face it, nobody wants to be in jail, not even the workers, but bills have to be paid, so the rest is history. A lot goes on in jail. People don't stop being who they are because they now find themselves in jail, especially a thief. Nobody likes a thief in jail because something always comes up missing, and it adds more confusion to a situation that is already in chaos. Most of the time in jail, when there is a problem on the block, it's usually because somebody is missing something, and that's one of the biggest forms of disrespect—going into somebody's cell and stealing something. That's a major violation among the incarcerated persons; just staring in an incarcerated person's cell can also bring you some problems. Believe it or not, officers have to deal with stealing also. We had an officer who took another officer's lunch out of the refrigerator and ate it. The officer started doing this on a regular basis until he was caught— talking about disrespect. Well, they gave this officer a deal he couldn't refuse, and his free lunch program was over, just like that. That takes a lot of nerve to do that; it could have ended with a show of hands, but no reason to get yourself in trouble because of a hungry thief.

The job can be difficult for a lot of different reasons. But everybody has a limit to what they are going to put up with. As a corrections officer, you will get provoked at some point in your career, but you have to maintain control over your emotions and never let them lead you out of character because they are testing you; however, you can be firm without being foolish. Not having self-control will definitely make your job harder or nonexistent if administration can prove you acted out of emotion and not within the description of your duties. The incarcerated persons, on the other hand, don't usually get time added to their sentence in jail unless they assaulted a corrections officer or were involved in a fight with a weapon, and someone was seriously injured.

Under normal circumstances, like a fight in jail or the incarcerated person was found with drugs, the incarcerated person would likely just get *keep-lock*—a term we use that says an incarcerated person will be locked in their cell for twenty-three hours per day until further notice. But, for the most part, respect has to exist between the officer and the incarcerated persons for things to run smoothly and efficiently in the jail. Unfortunately, fights happen in jail, assaults happen in jail, but it's officers' responsibility to be alert and involved, making sure the safety and security of the block are maintained.

In certain circles, people refer negatively to corrections officers as if they are some bad omen. But ask yourself a question: Would you rather be paid to go to jail or volunteer for free? I think I know what most people would pick, and I believe I've proved my point. Corrections is probably one of the most challenging jobs in law enforcement.

We don't carry guns inside the jail, batons (nightsticks), or any type of weapon. I know that on TV shows, officers are shown wearing nightsticks. However, in the real world, no weapons are carried by the officers. It's an honest living and an interesting job. Never a boring moment, and the pay is good, at least in the jail where I worked.

It's also a dangerous job; anything can happen at any time. In a split second, your whole life can change. The bottom line is, jail is not too different from everyday life in society. You still have to follow the rules or face the consequences for violating them, and that goes for the officers as well. History has shown me jail is not a one-way street. Officers can be easily walked out in handcuffs just like the incarcerated persons if they violate the rules and regulations that are enforced. It's not a job for everybody. There is an invisible line throughout the jail, and once an officer crosses that line, there is no coming back. So, before you take the job, ask yourself who you are. Because if you don't know who you are, the incarcerated persons are going to tell you who you're going to be. It's a lot of stress on the job, but don't let that stress lead to your arrest. There is no gray area in corrections; you're either going to do the right thing or not, and if you choose not to, then deal with the consequences and everything that comes with it.

By now, you can probably see the many similarities between the officer and the incarcerated persons in the jail environment. I must also point out that if you're a decent officer, the incarcerated persons will give you a heads-up if some nonsense is about to take place. To be an effective corrections officer, it's imperative that you have a good rapport with the majority of the incarcerated persons. The majority of them are respectful toward staff, but there are always a few who are determined to try and do things their way, and then they become very familiar with the rules and regulations and keep-lock.

As time goes on, both the officer and the incarcerated person realize that we can't attain a certain level of peace without both contributing to it. Nothing in life is perfect; everything on God's earth has flaws. However, to make some things work, it just takes effort and mutual respect from the officer and the incarcerated person.

As a corrections officer, your objective should be to stay alert, maintain security and safety, and don't become predictable where the incarcerated person knows when you are going to make your rounds and tries to time you, making you appear complacent.

We're not treated any better than the incarcerated persons in a lot of situations. Don't assume that just because you have on the same uniform as another officer that y'all are on the same team. I had a training officer tell an incarcerated person to go after me, as if that was part of my training, and it backfired on the officer and the incarcerated person. The officer had to run into the dayroom and abort that mission.

He then told me, "You're going to make it. You're going to be alright." I never trusted that officer after that day, and he was my training officer, a total idiot. After my training was over, I never spoke to him again in my career. I never did that to an officer in my entire career; I never understood why an officer would do something like that, plus how would he explain that if something had happened. Back when we came into the building, it was a lot different than it is now; it was overcrowded, dirty, hot, and the incarcerated person population was through the roof. I must say over the years, a lot of improvement has been made to the jail, and the pen is maintained much better now; it almost looks like a different place. I have a lot of memories walking those halls, some good, some not so good, but you figure it out and you keep going. Quitting wasn't an option because people were quitting every week.

I can only imagine if you're locked up how your mind can play tricks on you, especially when it comes to your personal life. Even for officers, your personal life can be a distraction to keeping your focus or being at your best when dealing with the work environment. You can think that despite what the jail is going through, you have to keep your focus and remember the problem is not with you; the problem is usually something they don't like about the system. We don't make the rules; we just enforce them, and that's where sometimes situations go left—the incarcerated person isn't having an issue with the officer; they have an issue with a part of the system the officer is trying to enforce. You can never take it personally, and that goes for both sides, the officer and the incarcerated persons.

Sometimes both sides want to be heard. The Jail clinic plays a very important role in the whole scheme of things. I don't think we could get past the week without a major disturbance if it weren't for the great job the nurses and doctors do in the jail. I feel the medical staff is just as important if not more important than the Department of Corrections staff. I have the utmost respect for the medical staff in the jail, especially for the professionalism in how they execute their jobs. I think it's just as dangerous to be on the medical staff as it is to be an officer because on occasion they are attacked too when all they are doing is trying to help someone. Again, I can't say enough about the respect I have for the medical staff all over this country who work in these jails; it's not easy. May God continue to bless you.

If the nurses and doctors didn't do their job, there would be way more tension and codes in the jail if they were lackadaisical in their duties. The medical staff has to work in the same dangerous toxic environment that we have to work in, and they get assaulted from time to time also, but they still show up to work and do their jobs professionally. I would say on the surface, the incarcerated persons have it worse in jail than the officers; however, we both suffer from the same side effects of being exposed to the jail. We have an abundance on both sides of the coin dealing with depression, and I'm sure a lot of cases go unreported because of the stigmas that accompany a diagnosis of depression, especially for the officer. I think just walking into the jail environment raises your anxiety level because of all that is going on at the same time and the unpredictability of what can occur.

I had actually thought I had seen it all in the streets of New York: the Bronx, Queens, Brooklyn, Harlem, and Manhattan. But I saw the aftermath of a fight in the penitentiary. We were responding to a code, and I was the second officer on the scene. There was an incarcerated person lying on the floor in a pool of blood that encircled his whole body. I had never seen that much blood come out of a person's body in my life. I thought he was dead; he was hit over the head with a metal chair. I had to appear unmoved because all eyes were on us at the time. I will never forget that; I learned weeks later he lived. Thank God. Just writing about it makes me nauseous. I also saw an incarcerated person who unfortunately hung himself. That was horrible also, but nothing compares to all that blood I saw that day. I also saw an incarcerated person cut so badly in the face you could see his teeth on the outside. It's not easy taking all that in and then going home around your family like nothing ever happened. I'm sure a lot of people who have worked in a jail for a few years have some horrible images they can't get out of their head.

Jail can be a very uncomfortable environment because you can catch a bad one no matter who you are if they catch you not paying attention. Every year in jails across the country, an officer is injured permanently or worse. Nobody who works there is immune from getting assaulted; anybody can get it. I have worked with a few officers who seemed scared to death, but after a while, they understand the environment and make the adjustment, and some just flat out quit. If you are not certain about something, ask. If it doesn't feel right, don't do it. Put safety first so you can't go wrong.

One day, an incarcerated person came to my block, and immediately, I smelled a horrible odor. The incarcerated person had a cast on his arm and told me he had been wearing that soggy cast for about three years because he hadn't seen a doctor since then. I called the clinic and informed them that I had an incarcerated person here with a cast on his arm that smelled terrible. When I sent him to the clinic, I was told that when they removed the cast, he had maggots all over his arm and the flesh was falling off. The visual picture turns my stomach. Whoever removed that cast, that image is burned in their mind forever. In jail, you never know what you are going to see, hear, or have to deal with on a daily basis.

People from all walks of life come to jail for many different reasons. No two incarcerated persons have the same experience. Jail has a way of showing you who is who just by being observant: watching if they go on visits, get packages and commissary, talk a lot on the phone, or receive mail. These things let you know if the incarcerated person is still connected to the outside world, or if nothing is happening, then it's a safe bet that no one really cares about them on the outside. Sometimes you don't know what's best because if you have it too good in jail, you don't mind coming back, I guess, and if you have it kind of hard in there, it makes you not want to return. I have seen incarcerated persons' cells look like a store with so much stuff: one hundred soups, fifty plastic bottles of soda, chips, candy, you name it. They had an abundance, but I also noticed that those who had it like that were not regular incarcerated persons who keep coming back; some you never see again in jail. It's obvious they have a life on the outside. I'm going to keep it one hundred; even though I'm from Mount Vernon, most of the incarcerated persons whose cells looked like a store were from Yonkers, and most of them never came back when they left. Just an observation.

I feel that corrections is a young person's game. At some point, you get too old for this routine, no matter if you are an officer or an incarcerated person. Everything in life has an expiration date, even life itself, so time is precious and valuable. We have to be smarter in how we spend our time because, let's face it, it's more valuable than money and gold. I think most environments come with a common-sense expiration date; it's different on different levels, but you know as an individual when it's time to pack it in, and at that point, if you don't leave, you're putting yourself and anybody depending on you to do your job, whether it's an officer or an incarcerated person, at risk.

I heard somebody once say nobody beats Father Time. Now I know exactly what they meant. If you live long enough, the body has a way of telling us, *I'm not doing that anymore*, and *What's the rush? So slow down*. And if we don't listen to our bodies, I think everybody is smart enough to know the consequences. Being exposed to jail for over twenty-five years will affect anybody. Something about you will change for sure. The jail is made of concrete and steel; that structure isn't going anywhere. I think it's safe to say the officer and the incarcerated person will wear out before the jail does.

When I started working for the Department of Corrections, I had a ten-year plan. Before I worked there, I was working two jobs and attending a local college in New Rochelle. I'm fourteen credits short of my bachelor's degree. I had planned to finish up at school and leave corrections, but life happened. I became distracted and mentally consumed by the job.

I'm sure that happens to a lot of us when you think about it because who wants to spend the rest of their lives in jail? Whether you're an officer or an incarcerated person, life dictates our destiny most of the time. And time flies, and you go in a totally different direction than the one you originally picked out for yourself. I think it's safe to say that jail has a far-reaching effect on both the officer and the incarcerated person. Jail is a place and an environment we both will never forget. I think if an incarcerated person doesn't come back to jail, I would say they turned a negative into a positive. Actually, it's a luxury the officer doesn't have. We signed up for twenty-five years; that's our agreement from the gate. The moment we take the job, it's a life sentence, and the person who started the job changes over the years, and you become a different person. I guess you can't help it because most of us get the job in our twenties, and we leave in our fifties.

Actually, if you didn't change, it wouldn't be considered normal because you are aging. Over a twenty-five-year time period, we all change; that's a part of life. We have a facility for female incarcerated persons, and a lot of men work over there. I used to think male officers shouldn't work with the female incarcerated persons; however, we had a male captain in the penitentiary who was accused of having an improper relationship with two male inmates. So after that occurred, I had to throw away my theory about male officers working with only male incarcerated persons out of the window. I realized it's not about the building you work in; it's the individual officer's mentality. If you're a degenerate officer, it doesn't matter what building you work in; it's going to be a problem either way.

Over the years, we have had officers in every building who have had inappropriate relationships with incarcerated persons, leading to their arrests.

You would think a person who goes home every day wouldn't have these problems, but like my father used to say, sometimes you just don't know what makes a person tick. I guess it takes all kinds. It's crazy what goes on in prisons all over the world. We had a male officer who attempted to give a bouquet of flowers to a female incarcerated person. How is that normal? That's a major red flag. However, this person still works there, and we have seen officers get fired for a lot less. We, as a department, are supposed to ensure the safety and security of the facility. Isn't that a breach of security? Jail is a world within a world. You see things and hear things, and most things you would not believe if you didn't see them with your own eyes. That's why I say stay alert because someone you're working with can bring you down quicker than anything, and that's why I also say, "Trust no one." When you feel like you can't trust the officer you're working with, you're in for a long shift.

The jail is stressful enough without contributing to what is already there. The level of stress a jail bestows on an officer and an incarcerated person is immeasurable. It has almost become a way of life. It's an environment where you expect the worst, and if anything less than that happens, you count your blessings. Because jail can become hell on your mind, body, and soul, every trap in the streets you can think of exists in the jail, and if you're not street-smart, you're going to be jail-dumb, and it goes downhill from there. That's a fact. I got a good education in the streets. I learned from the best, that's why I didn't get caught up in a lot of that jail nonsense that was going down. Thank God I dodged those bullets because my whole career, you hear about officers getting caught up in those traps, and it can happen to anybody, and it usually does, but I thank God I walked out with no jail baggage attached to my future. Whoever was praying for me, I appreciate it.

I remember I was on the job for about two months. I had just left the car wash in my new car and was driving up Baychester Avenue in the Bronx. An unmarked police car pulled me over at Pittman Avenue and Baychester. I had my two-year-old son Justin in the car with me at the time. At that time, two more unmarked cars boxed me in and got out of their cars. I asked the officer what's going on. He said give him a minute when they brought an old lady to my car, and she said, "Yeah, that's him," without really looking at me. The police then informed me that the lady was robbed and identified me as the robber. The cop said she made a positive ID of me. I told the cop I didn't rob anybody; I just came from the car wash. My car was still wet.

As I was talking to the officer, I overheard another officer request a tow truck for my car. At that point, the officer I was talking to asked me for my ID, so I pulled out my wallet, and he saw my badge. He said, "Let me see that." He asked me why I didn't say I was on the job, and I replied that I didn't think it was necessary until now. He went on and spoke to his partner and told the lady she made a mistake. The officers apologized and drove off. Had I not had that badge, I was on my way to Rikers Island for something I didn't do. This was a prime example of being in the wrong place at the wrong time. Thank God that situation didn't escalate. Growing up in the hood, many of my brothers and sisters don't get that benefit of the doubt. It's supposed to be innocent until proven guilty, but that's not always the case, especially in the hood.

They say time flies when you're having fun, so it must drag in jail because it's anything but fun. As an officer, I noticed that a lot of incarcerated persons didn't take their cases to trial, and I asked one incarcerated person why it appears that all incarcerated persons don't take their cases to trial; they cop out to an offer instead. And I was told that if you blow a trial (lose your case), your time is doubled or tripled in some cases. So even the guy who knows he is innocent is not taking any chances in court and chooses to cop out. When you lose your case, you get lost in the system. I was told this, but I'm not sure how accurate that information is though. However, I do hear a lot of the incarcerated persons confirming that outlook. Working in a jail gives you a different perspective than when you first started; it appears to be a very complicated system that has many different approaches to justice.

In the court system, you win some, you lose some, just like life. Same odds, but who is really ready, willing, and able to gamble with their freedom? Not many are willing to take that risk. But for some, just being in jail can be a major risk. As they say, I have a lot of "OPPS" here. I remember I was leaving a block, and I was between these two sliding doors. An incarcerated person was already there, and the captain was entering that area as well. The sliding glass door closed, and the northwest side was opening. Now it's me, the captain, and an incarcerated person in between the doors, and entering was another incarcerated person. However, as soon as both incarcerated persons saw each other, they immediately started swinging at each other.

One guy was pitching a shutout until the other incarcerated person pulled out a homemade knife and started poking the other guy. As he was stabbing the other incarcerated person, I attempted to grab the guy with the knife, and the captain grabbed me and said, "Wait until the response team gets here." So we had to watch this defense-less incarcerated person continue to get stabbed, and we couldn't do anything. I kind of understood the captain's point of view, but it just didn't feel right at the time because what would have happened if the incarcerated person was killed? Looking back, it probably was the right call, but I'm not sure if we could have broken it up. Who knows? Anyway, everybody lived through it, and nobody was seriously injured.

Being locked up in that environment is very stressful for the officer and the incarcerated person. You never know what's going to happen from one minute to the next, and the anticipation leaves you in suspense until something actually occurs. If you pay enough attention, somebody will give you a clue that it's about to pop off because not everybody in jail wants to fight. And if you can get out in front of it before it happens, you save yourself a lot of non-sense and paperwork and hopefully help someone avoid an injury. Because at the end of the day, both the officer and the incarcerated person want peace, but sometimes the road to peace leads you down Confusion Street and Chaos Avenue.

I can't write this book without acknowledging two of the best union presidents and vice presidents in my career, Tommy O'Neill and Robert Delbene. When they worked together, they were the best we ever had. They used to come into our briefings to inform us what's going on with the building and the position the union is taking. They did it with passion and professionalism. They were probably the best duo in the history of correction officers' unions (in our facility, at least). They made you feel like somebody was actually fighting for your rights and benefits. They helped to balance out the craziness on the job. I have not seen them since I retired, but I hope wherever they are, they are enjoying life to the fullest with their families. God bless them; we are still benefiting from their hard work. I thank them for a job well done. I hope the president who is there now gets the same accolades when the officer retires under his watch, in unity. I wrote this book to illustrate with words and show how a jail affects the officer and the incarcerated person almost in the exact same way. I also spoke about some of the pitfalls and traps that officers fall into. Now there is no excuse for saying, "I didn't know." I hope this book can get the attention of somebody to affect change in the Department of Corrections.

The officers who dedicate twenty years or more across this country deserve better. Let's collectively turn the situation around because we can't continue to ignore the premature deaths of so many officers and the suicides and the families of our Department of Corrections brothers and sisters. Most of the officers are dying of heart attacks, strokes, high blood pressure, suicides, alcoholism—you name it. This is by no means normal. I'm sure something can be done to lighten the load for the officer so they don't feel so overwhelmed when health concerns and more problems knock on their door. Working for the Department of Corrections isn't just a job; it's a journey. It almost feels like a real-life game of dodgeball. But instead of getting hit with the ball, you get hit with life.

Sometimes the hit takes you out of the game of life, sometimes it doesn't, but we are all trying to make it to the finish line. Hey, it's not easy—if everybody could do it. Maybe the officers need to independently research this situation and find out how we can add years to our lives because the current system in place is subtracting, and we can't live with that, literally. Growing up in the hood, you hear all types of stories about jail—what to do, what not to do when you find yourself in one. If I had to give advice to a young person coming up now in the streets, I would say anything that might lead you to jail, stop doing it now because jail is not what you want. Take my word for it.

As I reflect on my twenty-five-plus-year career, it was definitely a journey and a learning experience. From the outside looking in, it appears that the Department of Corrections is one big happy family, everybody on the same page. But I have seen officers throw each other under the bus like they are part-time mechanics. Imagine that—you think the person you're working with has your back, and they flip on you like a flapjack (pancake). I'm not being paranoid when I say don't trust anyone; I have seen too many officers get stabbed in the back (not literally) by their so-called coworkers, and now you're supposed to be comfortable working with an individual who assisted in getting his last partner fired? I'm not blaming the officer because the other officer got fired, but I feel, why make a bad situation worse? That's why I live by the motto "Don't trust anybody." To be honest, finding a decent human being nowadays is like finding a needle in a haystack. Either something is real or fake; there's no such thing as "something is almost real."

You have some people in the Department of Corrections that you really can't trust. They come around you only to eavesdrop and get information, and then go back and tell somebody you probably are not cool with, just to start some nonsense or trying to use you as a pawn so they can advance. In the streets, they call it a sucker move. That happens a lot in jail. We all know this new incarcerated person culture is notorious for throwing one another under the bus for a shorter stay at the jail bed-and-breakfast. But officers, believe it or not, do it also for a lot of different reasons. But the bottom line is, you really can't trust anybody—that's a fact. I used to think some people on the job were antisocial, but after working there for a few years, they were my idols. They saw the deceitful playing field before I did. They did their time and left out of there before anyone noticed—a very smart move. I admire them for that. Enjoy your retirement, wherever you all may be.

I see a lot of ex-officers and officers still employed by the Department of Corrections, and the narrative pretty much has stayed the same. When I run into them on the streets, they always say the place has changed drastically, and there are always more rules to treat the incarcerated persons better. I hear that officers are now required to call the incarcerated persons *residents*, and now I'm hearing the jail resembles a hotel more than a jail. But there are always new memos or rules coming out on how we can best serve the incarcerated persons while the disrespect of officers and the ongoing assaults on staff continue without being addressed.

I have always wondered why the officers, who are almost always exposed to the detrimental elements from running the jail, are never considered when the powers that be make up the rules and regulations for operating the jail. Why aren't there more mandates implemented to give correctional staff more protection under the law? Instead, officers continue to get injured, some suffering career-ending injuries, and most of the time nothing happens to the incarcerated person who caused the injury. The playing field is definitely not a smooth one. If an officer does anything to protect themselves, it's almost always investigated; however, when an incarcerated person causes injury to the correctional officer, there is nothing in place that protects the officer. Administration is quick to tell you when an incarcerated person's rights have been violated, but what about the officers? Aren't their lives worth something every year, no matter what jail you're talking about?

Several officers receive permanent injuries from trying to do their job, which is not only devastating to the officers, but their whole family is affected by the situation as well. But year after year, memo after memo, officers get informed how to best treat the incarcerated persons and make them more comfortable. There is nothing written to give the officer more relief, mentally or physically, when doing their job. It's so one-sided. I'm surprised more officers are not getting injured on their posts because, remember, they are only human. And as horrible as the environment is, the officers are the only ones punished for not following the rules to the letter. The incarcerated person appears almost untouchable, no pun intended. You always hear about how they have rights, but what about the officer? Don't they have rights too? So why is there such a disparity in respect when it comes to the officer and incarcerated person? Why are officers still getting splashed with urine and feces, and nothing happens to the incarcerated person who initiated it? They need a law to protect the officers because throwing human bodily fluids at an officer should be a new charge because that's beyond disrespect; nobody should have to deal with that.

How come overtime posts are assigned based on who the officer is related to rather than on the officer's job longevity and earned merit? On the surface, the Department of Corrections appears to run like clockwork, but behind the scenes, it's a totally different story that's not favorable to the average officer. It's disheartening to see supervisors assigning women to certain blocks where most of the men can't even work. I'm almost positive that if their daughters, wives, or mothers worked there, they wouldn't post them on those blocks. So what makes these female officers different? I'm curious about what happened to common courtesy. I understand it's an equal-opportunity employment where we're not supposed to consider gender, but common sense should override some situations in jail that appear quite obvious.

For most officers, from the first day they walk into that jail, life as they remember it changes somewhat because a lot of different things officers have to put up with wouldn't be the same scenario if they were in a different environment. The level of disrespect in jail is off the charts, and if officers don't police themselves properly, they could find themselves in conflicts every day with both sides of the coin: officers and incarcerated persons. In my observation, I saw more officers disrespecting each other way worse than any incarcerated person was doing, outside of splashing an officer with urine. I stayed away from all that nonsense because it just adds to the problem and doesn't provide a solution. I can't tolerate disrespect, no matter where it's coming from.

In my opinion, too much of officers' personal business floats around the jail, and it becomes serious real quick. I don't have to tell you how serious it can get because mostly everybody already knows. However, it is what it is, and it's going to be what it's going to be. I remember an incarcerated person who would tell me stuff concerning other officers, and I would say to myself how and where did they get that information; but as time goes by, you realize the information you received from the incarcerated persons was, in fact, accurate. Jail is a lot like the streets—same problems, same situations, same people creating drama, just on a smaller scale. Sometimes it feels like the officers are trying to be like the incarcerated persons, and the incarcerated persons are trying to be like the officers—not all but some.

During my career, I have seen all walks of life walking down that hallway: rappers, ex-NBA players, R&B singers, lawyers, doctors—almost any profession you can think of. But once they put on that orange suit, I look at them no differently than I would any other incarcerated person who comes through our facility. I could probably write a book just about that alone if I wanted to, but I don't like to name-drop. However, we had officers jeopardizing their jobs trying to cater to the needs and wants of these so-called celebrities. I never could understand why you would put yourself in a position to get fired to cater to somebody you don't know or probably won't see again in life. You can't be an officer and at the same time be starstruck because it doesn't work like that. The worst thing you can do as an officer is play favoritism among the incarcerated persons— at that point, you have probably lost your block and, eventually, your job.

So is it really worth it? God bless the child who has their own. I used to hear officers trying to brag about who they used to hang out with like that's something to impress somebody with. When did it become cool to be a groupie? This new generation is something else. We all have a past. Nobody I know was born a correction officer or an incarcerated person. Too many people are playing make-believe.

This new generation thinks that going to jail automatically makes you a gangster. If you weren't a gangster before you went to jail, then you probably aren't one now. Knock it off. As an officer, twenty-five years in a jail can have an effect on anybody exposed to that environment for that long. It's not like any other job in law enforcement. It's almost like for twenty-five years, you're forced to live in an environment that's unlike anything you have ever seen or will ever see, and hopefully, you get to look back on your whole career and thank God you were one of the few who made it through. God bless all my brothers and sisters who have been subjected to the jail environment, and hopefully, the day comes when they never have to go back there again.

Most good officers were probably one incident away from being an incarcerated person themselves, growing up in the hood. Anything can happen to anybody at any time growing up in the hood, but you have to have a certain level of street smarts to move smoothly in the jail. Now, I'm not saying an officer has to be a thug in training to do his or her job, but you have to know about that life. It helps.

Jail is almost nothing like the average person thinks it is. Someone who frequents jail can easily distort the picture of how jail is when they discuss it with people who have not been and have no affiliation with incarceration. Jail requires a great deal of discipline on both sides. Individuals can get real reckless with their mouth over absolutely nothing. Most of the time, you have to really think before you speak because words are like bullets in jail—once they come out the barrel of your mouth, you can't put them back. I have seen incarcerated persons do it and corrections officers do it; it's never a good look no matter who does it. On the other hand, jail is necessary. Yes, indeed, in my twenty-five years as a corrections officer, I have observed individuals who definitely need to be inside some type of facility, getting some type of help. Perhaps they are dealing with a mental illness of some kind or some other situation that brings them too much negative attention, and they will hurt themselves and others with their behavior and their total disregard for the law and those who enforce it.

Just imagine spending eight hours or even sixteen hours dealing with a person totally out of control, smearing human feces all over themselves and daring you to come into their cell. That's the day of a correction officer. How are you going to deal with that? It's far from easy, but believe it or not, eventually you will get used to it; it just becomes another day at the jail. I will also point out that not all officers are exposed to this dilemma; some hide behind a last name or being a relative of somebody in charge, or they just cater to the supervisors so they don't get put in harm's way. I worked blocks my whole career because I enjoyed it; I like being around people.

I remember an officer told me to apply for a position in booking. I saw more energy at a funeral home than booking. I was like, thanks but no thanks, especially when I saw how a lot of officers were moving in that place, trying to survive. Some people will do anything to get a good post. It's embarrassing how low some will go.

Everybody who retires doesn't leave with dignity. We may all wear the same uniform in the jail, but those of us who wear it with integrity, that's what separates us from the others. Every officer in jail knows a few officers who will do anything to stay out of the blocks and get a good post; it's not a secret. Everybody knows who they were; most officers could rattle off names if they had to. When we first started, there was so much going on; you didn't really know what to do or focus on. Every day there was something new to deal with, aside from the circus-like atmosphere we inherited from day one. It was straight chaos from the gate, and it appeared some officers just chose to ignore it or were so preoccupied with the job that they didn't notice the other theatrics that were going on all over the jail.

Looking back, it's a miracle more officers didn't quit, because it was a correctional officer's nightmare dealing with what we had to deal with. I'm going to be completely honest: when I first started the job, it was worse than being in the streets because the level of disrespect was at an all-time high. As a rookie, you don't really know how to respond to that. In the streets, you already know how it's going to play out, but in the jail, you have to color inside the lines and operate on a professional level, not an emotional one, if you want to stay employed. On both sides of the fence, people say things to you in jail they would never say in the streets, especially back then when we were twenty-five years younger. At this age, you can't entertain it because nobody's trying to spend their retirement behind bars over some straight-up foolishness. As you get older, you are supposed to get smarter. If that's not happening with you, it's safe to say you're going in the wrong direction.

I knew a lot of people who were in jail when I first started. But I was focused from day one because being from Mount Vernon and working in the jail is not an automatic cakewalk for the officers. For whatever reason, a lot of officers from Mount Vernon don't make it. And when you lose your job, who's going to pay your bills? Nobody. Then they're going to act like they don't know you. They say, "Don't start nothing, won't be nothing." Twenty-five years later, either you crossed the finish line or you just finished. And with corrections, you almost never get a do-over, so you have to move intelligently and cautiously because one mistake can stop you even before you really get started. And all of your training, physically and mentally, will be all for nothing.

I could be wrong, and it's only my opinion, but it's always "could be worse" considering what goes on in other jails. For the most part, most of the officers and the incarcerated persons vibe with one another. It's probably not 100 percent, but the majority rules, which makes things a lot smoother and peaceful. Overall, my twenty-five-year career was interesting. I don't miss the place; I miss some of the people.

I bumped into an officer a few months back who I remembered worked in the pen. He had been retired for over fifteen years, and he was totally angry about a situation that happened over fifteen years ago in the pen, and he acted like it just happened. I was confused as to why he is still walking around with that stress from fifteen years ago; that can't be healthy. Then I thought, Is this related to why so many officers have heart attacks carrying stress baggage from the job? This officer was adamantly angry, even though it was fifteen years ago. I think it's normal to be in that abnormal environment for twenty-five years and have a number of negative images committed to memory; that's a part of the job you will never be retired from. But hopefully, you manage to work around it and not allow that twenty-five years on the job to rob you of hopefully another twenty-five years going forward.

CHAPTER 2

I remember when I first started working in the Department of Corrections twenty-five years ago. I felt like it was too far away to think about a milestone only a handful of us would get to experience. And as I've reflected on those years gone by, where did the time go? Now it feels like time flew by, twenty-five years gone just like that. A lot has happened in those twenty-five years. We have not only spent twenty-five years of our lives in jail but also have lost coworkers, family, friends, and some associates. They say time heals all wounds, but some people can never be replaced; their passing leaves a void that can never be filled.

Looking back on my years in the Department of Corrections, going forward, health is my number one concern. It's the only thing of real importance in the whole scheme of things besides your kids and spouse. I know some people like to feel important walking around in that jail, but no job inside that jail is going to take more than twenty minutes to replace you (trust and believe) when you're gone. So with that being said, when it's your last day on the job and you don't have to ever put that uniform back on, I pray you leave that place as healthy as you were when you came in there, or what was it all for? Because nobody sees the big picture.

But look at how many officers don't make it to retirement, or right after retirement, they expire. We have lost a lot of officers throughout the years, so many that now it feels like a Department of Corrections annual event. I know death is a part of life, but we lose a lot of officers year after year, and old age is seldom the reason. In my travels, I have run into a lot of retired and active corrections officers who are dealing with several health issues they didn't have prior to getting the job.

Working in the jail is a hard job. It's unpredictable, dangerous, and your career could be over in a split second from a number of different circumstances. And I don't think anybody has to tell you how dangerous it is to be an incarcerated person. I think it's safe to say whether you are an officer or an incarcerated person, your health can very well be affected by your exposure to the jail. Probably on average, an incarcerated person is assaulted every day in jail, although it almost always goes unreported because the incarcerated persons think it's a form of snitching. However, we all know that the no-snitching policy is only to exploit someone's gullibility and inexperience of the streets—because nobody in their right mind is going to take a jail sentence for something they didn't do or allow someone to victimize them and remain silent because it's the respectful thing to do when someone blatantly disrespects you. Doesn't that sound crazy? For what? So a few people who don't even matter say, on occasion, that you kept it real. Keep those empty, worthless accolades; I don't need them. Life is too short for me to care about what the word on the street is. I'm committed to my immediate family; that's the only vote that matters to me.

Jail brings out the worst in some people. A lot of games are being played in jail, and somebody is always being set up, whether it's an officer or an incarcerated person. People change behind that wall. You can't trust anyone you think you know but you really don't. What is the officers' code they live by when they have problems in the blocks, and some officers are being extorted? You never hear that being reported. Why is that? There isn't a "no snitching" rule among officers, so why isn't it reported when they are being extorted and sometimes assaulted in their blocks? A lot has changed now over the years. The blatant disrespect for female officers is on the rise. Long before I retired, it started feeling more like a jail to the officers than it does to the incarcerated persons.

Throughout this book, I have attempted to show the similarities between officers and incarcerated persons, although the jail seems more restrictive to the officers than the incarcerated persons. I know it's impossible to put my entire twenty-five-year career in one book, but I'm going to try to include the events that really got my attention. I didn't socialize that much with my coworkers, but early in my career, I went on a fishing trip with about thirty officers. Things were going good until an officer got drunk and climbed on top of the boat and started urinating on an officer below (where I'm from, we don't play like that). The officer who was urinated on grabbed the officer who urinated on him and commenced to giving that officer an old-fashioned Brooklyn beatdown. Even after the fighting was over, officers started throwing everything that wasn't nailed down overboard. The captain called the Coast Guard, who escorted our boat back to the dock in New Rochelle, Glen Island. I never went on another fishing trip. That was one of the most ridiculous things I have ever seen. The officer who urinated on the other officer was fired about two years later for an unrelated incident. Not surprised.

Now, looking back on that incident and a few others, I don't know who had more fights: officers against officers or incarcerated persons against incarcerated persons. Every week, you would hear about two officers fighting, and sometimes it would be two female officers fighting. It's almost funny that we're supposed to enforce a code of conduct that most of us can't even live by. I'm not saying all officers were auditioning for Mike Tyson's old job, but it was enough to take notice. Where else do you find employees fighting amongst themselves almost on a daily basis? Like I said, how can you enforce a rule you are finding it difficult to live by yourself? And this was happening almost on a regular basis. It's been alleged that a sergeant took an officer into the bathroom and beat the living crap out of him. How do you allow somebody to put their hands on you, and you don't do anything? I guess they know who to hit and who is not going for it. Disrespect runs thick in the jail, and it doesn't come from the incarcerated persons either. Some people think their job title allows them to get away with disrespect toward officers. It's a shame, but nobody should have to tolerate disrespect, not the incarcerated persons nor the officers. That's why I say the jail environment is just as chaotic for the officers as it is for the incarcerated persons.

Nobody is living their best life in jail. We had an officer who appeared to have a nervous breakdown because of his interaction with the supervisor. What exactly happened, no one knows for sure, but the officer was laid out on the floor, and he wasn't breakdancing. The jail can be a stressful environment at times for a number of reasons, and most of the time, it has nothing to do with the incarcerated persons or the job. In my career, I have talked a few officers out of going after another officer over some disrespectful thing that they did or said. Jail is like high school all over again, where people think they get a do-over because they didn't turn up in high school. That ship sailed. Let it go, it's over.

Don't get me wrong; it's not an exclusive event where only the officers are disrespected. I had a female supervisor come to my post on the verge of tears, explaining to me how awfully she was being treated by her peers. I could see the pain and the stress in her face with every word she uttered about her ordeal. Part of me felt sorry for her that a human being could be made to feel this way by other human beings, and another part of me was angry she wasn't getting the respect and professional courtesy she deserved. She is no longer with us, but I pray she has found peace in eternal paradise, and she will never have to endure that level of discomfort and disrespect again.

In jail, it's a very thin line between an officer and an incarcerated person. Now, I'm not saying officers are doing anything illegal. I'm just saying neither is ever given the benefit of the doubt when something happens in the jail; we probably use more lawyers than the incarcerated persons. Throughout your career as an officer, you will need a lawyer for almost everything, from calling in sick too much to how you perform your duties at work. It's not a good feeling, but it's the system that's in place that an officer has to deal with. Officers get charges just like incarcerated persons, and it's just as stressful as an incarcerated person being charged with something. The stress is real in jail; incarcerated persons stressed about their cases, their family, and a number of things that have the incarcerated person stressed. And you always have those same officers worried about where they're going to work, why they were put on that post, or something totally unrelated to jail, which is usually worse, and the saga continues.

The minor block was a nightmare for some officers; they would go to the emergency rooms before they would go to the minor block and work. The minors would flood the blocks about twice a week with their toilets: they stuff clothes in the toilet and just keep flushing until you have four feet of water on the block. I will admit the minor block was a disaster waiting to happen or already in progress back in the day. There was always drama on the minor block.

Officers and incarcerated persons go through hell in the jail, perhaps for different reasons, but at the end of the day, stress is a two-way street. I know most people would think that the majority of officers' stress comes from the incarcerated persons, but nothing could be farther from the truth. Most of an officer's stress comes from administration or other officers. There is always a certain level of drama being entertained somewhere in the jail, or post changes, just to name a few things that could stress an officer out and disrupt their whole week, month, or career.

Unfortunately, I have witnessed the jail environment reduce people whom I have known to be strong mentally and physically to almost a shell of themselves compared to how they used to be. In some situations, it's sad. To others, it's embarrassing to allow a place to break you down like that, where you no longer even attempt to stand up for yourself but fall for all the bullcrap that is thrown your way. Nobody in jail invented the wheel or created the vaccine for COVID; nobody there can walk on water or tell you what the future of the world is going to be. So I think it's safe to say everybody there is basically in the same boat or, more appropriately, the same jail. What I mean by that is we are all in jail. There is no reason to glorify anybody or vilify them because of their situation in jail or their position in the department.

As an officer, you see up close and personal how a jail operates. I don't know how it is now, but when I was there, the block officers, the booking officers, and ERT helped keep things running smoothly. It's not an easy job by no means, and if you have the wrong people around you, an eight-hour shift can feel like a week. But I mostly had good partners to work with, so we seldom had a problem. I could be wrong, but most of my experience in jail has been that if you treat a person with respect, most of the time, they will give you that same respect in return. However, on occasion, you will come across a person who is totally irrational, but that's the job—take the good with the bad. We had some good people to work with, and we had some walking liabilities to deal with also.

We had an officer who would hit the code in advance, wait until help arrives, then start trying to have a confrontation with the incarcerated person. This particular officer got officers suspended, lost wages, and lost vacation time because they were his partner at the time. This officer was a straight clown who belonged in a circus, not a jail. His job was saved on several occasions by the union. The moral of that story: good union, terrible officer.

No matter what you experience in jail as an officer, write it the way you saw it, not what somebody tells you to write. We had an officer who saved his job when everybody else got fired because he wrote the report and didn't and wouldn't change it for anybody. Don't allow somebody already in a jam to jam you because you think you know an officer or a person. You might be surprised what some of them will do for a good post, a day off, or just to hang out in the captain's office. They will spill their guts about everything they think they know to get a good overtime spot. It's just a shame how some of these officers move. I have seen officers and incarcerated persons flip-flop under pressure like they were a gymnast, and most of the time, it's not that serious. Working with the wrong person, you can find yourself doing more time than some of the incarcerated persons you're paid to watch.

I had a few good partners. My best partner was in the med unit. We worked well together. May God bless him and his family. The worst officer I ever worked with was on the 1K block in the jail. He had to be the worst officer in the corrections officer history. He was fired eventually, and the building became safer overnight because of his firing. That was one time I can honestly say that the administration got it right.

Stress is a big part of the jail. It's going to visit you on the job no matter who you are, eventually. Some of us handle stress better than others, and some officers turn to alcohol or worse to deal with that manufactured stress from the job, which is only going to make things worse. And nothing is more dangerous than working with an officer who is distracted by the elements his or her stress has caused. Everybody deals with what they observe as stress differently. Some are good at managing the stress brought on by the jail, and some people turn their life upside down. But one thing is certain: it's something we all have to deal with. Alcohol consumption outside of moderation is definitely becoming a nemesis to an officer's career. I have seen so many officers fired for alcohol-related infractions in my twenty-five-year career, it's unbelievable. The numbers are beyond what you can imagine. My question: What's being done to help those officers before it gets out of hand? Because nobody can convince me that the jail environment is not partially to blame.

I once worked with an officer who appeared so intoxicated he went to sleep in a vacant bed we had in the dorm area. He was supposed to be my help for the day. I hope it's not still like that now because that can cause problems for both of you. Don't get me wrong, most of the officers are decent, hardworking individuals. But we do have some officers who didn't really know they were officers or just didn't care. A sense of humor is a must in that environment because you have to laugh to keep yourself from losing your mind. One thing about jail: everything can be going smoothly one minute, and the next, all hell can break loose. A lot of times, you have three seconds to make the right decision, and you won't realize if you're right or wrong until weeks later when you could possibly get written up because of the way you handled the situation. You're never 100 percent sure.

I remember the first time I escorted an incarcerated person to the psychiatrist. He had come from upstate prison after doing ten years and came down on an appeal. As soon as we walked into the psychiatrist's office, the incarcerated person recognized the psychiatrist and immediately became agitated and loud. He started walking aggressively toward the psychiatrist, and I stepped in between them, telling the incarcerated person to calm down as it's not worth it. The incarcerated person then started saying that this psychiatrist wrote an unfavorable report to the courts during his sentencing. I stood between them and told him, "Let's go," without hesitation. He complied, and we left the psychiatrist's office. About an hour later, I was told to go to the captain's office. The captain wanted to see me. I walked into the captain's office, and the psychiatrist had called the captain and told him I had saved his life by stepping in between the two of them. That situation could have gone wrong from the start. I saw that same incarcerated person a week later, and he thanked me for not letting him get in any trouble and possibly ruining his chances for his appeal.

Officers and incarcerated persons get written up regularly in jail. When I really think about it, the officers are probably written up more than the incarcerated persons. Officers lose vacation days, get suspended, and sometimes can even be fired for being written up. When the incarcerated person gets written up, they may lose some good time, or depending on the write-up, they may face outside charges. But in my twenty-five years of being in the jail, the officers appeared to be charged more frequently and severely than the incarcerated persons. It almost feels like a no-win situation for the officer because the repercussions for a bad report can appear endless, and your immediate options and alternatives are usually gloomy and grim at best.

After twenty-five years of working in the jail, the average officer has been through some things and has seen things. Especially the firing of a lot of officers in a twenty-five-year span speaks volumes. When you have a serious debate on who has it worse in jail, the officers or the incarcerated persons, nobody can say with certainty which side has it the worst. But I think I made my point with the question because it shouldn't be debatable, but it is. I don't even know if being a sergeant is that much better because I know several officers who went back to being an officer after they were promoted to sergeant. That position has some issues, obviously, as well. What they are exactly, I don't know.

But I do know how difficult it is to retire from the jail without feeling stressed out, mentally exhausted, and physically depleted. Just walking out of that place after retirement is a blessing not a lot of officers are fortunate enough to experience. Personally, I feel like the job drains you mentally and physically, and the things you have to endure on an almost daily basis add danger on top of that. It amazes me what some people get away with on that job and what some people have to go through for what looks like something minor, to say the least. I remember hearing about an officer using the bathroom and leaving his gun behind in the bathroom, only to be found by a civilian. Imagine if that weapon got into the wrong hands. Also, we had an officer discharge his weapon in the lobby of the jail. How dangerous is that? You're in the lobby, and a bullet is ricocheting off the walls—not really an ideal situation to be in. But what's ironic about both situations is that both officers were promoted, if you can believe that. I know officers who have been fired for a lot less. I understand accidents happen, but these accidents could have cost somebody their life. It's a dangerous enough job without these guns being misplaced and misused. When you think about it, it's beyond scary. It just goes to show favoritism can become fatal.

You can't be too careful in jail because being careless can cost lives. When you are appointed to a position you have never worked before, it's not just dangerous for the person working the post, it's dangerous for anybody near that post. I never understood how you get to supervise blocks when you never worked blocks in your entire career. I saw that a lot. It's like getting the bat boy at Yankee Stadium to pitch in the World Series—sounds like a disaster in the making to me. I thank God no one was hurt in those incidents, and they probably were mistakes; but if a civilian did the same thing, I wonder what and how it would be approached. I feel like jail should be a safe place for an officer or an incarcerated person. Unfortunately, it's not. Jail is where anything can happen at any time. Incarcerated persons will use most anything to make a weapon, and judging by some of the weapons we manage to confiscate during searches of blocks, they are very creative. The more I think about it, the more it feels like a department within the department.

Especially when there is a problem in one of the blocks or somewhere in the building, certain officers don't even concern themselves with what's going on. Imagine working in the jail, and you're totally ignoring the incarcerated persons' or civilians' requests for help. How do you live with yourself seeing one of your coworkers being assaulted, and you do nothing? It's a lot more dangerous in the building than we think because of officers who made a career out of looking the other way. They should have been crossing guards, not jail guards; I guess they applied for the wrong job. I know we are not supposed to use the term *jail guards*, but some officers really have not earned the title *correctional officers*; that's just my opinion. I wrote the book to show the many similarities of the officers and the incarcerated persons; however, I can't help but write about things that also caught my attention while I was there. So if I go off on a tangent every now and then, I apologize; some things I just have to get out of my system.

I remember when I first started the job, an officer got splashed by an incarcerated person with a cup of urine. I never found out what happened exactly because the officer was a good officer; he wasn't a troublemaker. I was surprised to see him walking off his post with piss all over his shirt. We also had a supervisor that was hit in the face with feces as he was walking through the blocks. To me, that's beyond disrespect, or maybe the incarcerated person is an undiagnosed mental patient because to remain professional after something like that is a stretch; everybody has their limits. I always say the officers in the blocks are on the front lines because they have to deal with the problem long before the ERT (emergency response team) gets there. Five minutes in a block that has a problem can feel like two hours, so you have to mentally prepare yourself for the worst and go from there and hope that it can be resolved quickly. The jail, for the most part, runs smoothly, but it has its moments.

When I first started, there were no body alarms, no ERT, not even a whistle, just two security phones to call in a code. Through the years, they implemented ERT (emergency response team). The pioneers of ERT took their jobs very seriously. However, I heard just recently that they allowed an officer to join ERT who allegedly failed the physical a few times, and I'm being told this person couldn't do twenty-five push-ups if his life depended on it. It's obviously not like it was back in the day if this is true. Imagine you waiting for the ERT to respond and this person slowing down the team. Not really a good scenario when you have a major problem on your block. The incarcerated persons and the officers are affected by this dilemma. Nobody wants to hear, "Help is on the way," when somebody could be getting seriously injured, officers included.

I started my career in the penitentiary, and I remember the supervisors used to say in our briefings that they were going to send officers to the jail like you're supposed to be scared. I volunteered to go to the jail because I liked the challenge. I can honestly say I didn't see a big difference, but the pen was a little calmer, but not by much. I guess they were already sentenced and not trying to lose any good time in the pen. I really wish I had gone sooner, but I enjoyed my time in the jail. We had some good supervisors in the pen, and we had some good supervisors in the jail also. However, at midnight shifts in the jail, we had a supervisor who was totally out of bounds with a lot of people. All I will say is that karma is undefeated if you know what I mean. I learned that the best thing you can have on your side in jail is patience. Don't rush anything. Everything will come to you in time; you just have to take your time. Before you know it, all the questions you have will be answered. That's a fact. After a few years on the job, you won't have any more speculations going on. It will be all facts and the old adage "Time will tell" applies to jail perfectly.

There's one thing about jail that's very noticeable: the environment preys on the weak. It doesn't matter if you're an officer or an incarcerated person, medical staff, or civilian worker. If you have a timid nature, the jail will eat you up and spit you out. Like I said before, be yourself, and I said this a few times already, the job is not for everybody. I have seen officers and incarcerated persons get caught up pretending they are somebody else, just saying *no* so you don't get caught up in no nonsense, and your six months can turn into six years just by being involved in something you have no business being involved in, all because you couldn't say no. It works in the streets too! If you had to pick an attribute that everyone should have in the jail so things could go smoother, it's their communication skills. Not everybody has them, however. The key to understanding is communication. I feel comprehension plays a big part also because if you don't understand what's being articulated, that brings us back to square one.

OK, getting back to the subject, when I think about it, it appears more officers get hurt in the jail than incarcerated persons. I think the jail environment is more dangerous for the officers than the incarcerated person, especially since the officer almost never sees it coming. I can't begin to count the number of officers who sustained permanent injuries and scars just from doing their job. And a lot of these injuries are career-ending, which changes the officers' entire life forever and their families. Every day a correction officer goes to work unbeknownst to him, it could very well be his last day on the job because of a severe injury. It's a dangerous job that we do without a weapon, no baton (nightstick), no Mace or pepper spray, or stun guns, and everything in the jail is made of steel and concrete. In a lot of posts, it's just you and the incarcerated persons and your street smarts and your academy training ability—good luck with that. And it's all fun and games until someone gets hurt; nothing humorous about that.

Sometimes jail feels like an intimidation contest, an ice-grilling contest. The minors are trying to be baby gangsters, and some of the adults are trying to convince the population they're tough. Someone is always trying to test another incarcerated person or even the officers on some blocks. It can feel like a constant vibe of negativity for some reason. You have to block a lot of that nonsense out, or you just could get into major problems. Officers have to always remember most incarcerated persons don't have anything to lose except good time, but the officer stands to lose their job and everything that comes with it if provoked to operate out of character and your job description. So you need to stay alert and focused. And also remember, nobody in their right mind wants all that drama in jail; plus it's corny and totally unnecessary. You see so much crazy stuff in jail it's not even funny. I don't know why people go to jail and automatically think they have to turn it up; that behavior played out like the high top fade.

Over the years, I have seen so many officers get fired for trying to bring in contrabands to somebody they know from the outside. Nobody who is cool with you is going to ask you to bring in anything, and if y'all were cool, that friendship is over as soon as they ask you for something. Why risk your job to cater to a person who doesn't have good intentions for you? It's not worth it. Save your job; lose that friend. I remember an officer from the academy was working in the female unit and became involved with a female incarcerated person. While she was locked up, I heard he was bringing her stuff in, and when she was released, she kicked him to the curb. This officer lost his job, his family, and his home all because he lost his focus. I remember him being a nice guy in the academy with little or no street smarts, apparently. And he is not the only one who went that route. Every now and then, you would hear of an officer or supervisor getting into trouble in the female unit. It's their right to work there, but it doesn't look right for them to work there. It's not worth it. Just my opinion. An officer can get falsely accused of something in the female unit, and that stigma will be attached to his name his whole career and beyond. Why take that chance? Like I said, it's just my opinion.

In today's workplace, you have to be careful. Something as innocent as giving someone a compliment can have you in the warden's office facing departmental charges. If your compliment is taken the wrong way, the safest bet is to keep everything professional. I have seen several officers get into trouble. I don't know the entire story on any of those cases, but it was along those lines that something inappropriate may have been said. That's where things are drastically divided because an incarcerated person can clearly be disrespectful toward female officers or supervisors, and almost nothing ever happens. But an officer can just be accused of using improper rhetoric toward female staff, and it's almost with absolute certainty departmental charges will follow. I guess I worked there too long because I totally understand it. If an incarcerated person is already facing a boatload of time, what's a Department of Corrections write-up to them compared to his outside charges? However, there has to be some kind of deterrent put in place because to do nothing is only going to create bigger problems in the future.

OK, enough of beating that dead horse. We have a saying: "The walls have ears," meaning no matter what you say in jail, regardless of the conversation, someone is ear hustling. And officers wonder how their business is all over the building. Most of the time, your conversation leaves the block before you do. Officers forget sometimes they are actually in a jail. We received a memo that said that all personal property should remain in your locker or your car. Actually, they should add to it all personal conversations should remain out of the jail. I remember when I was there, we would wait until we got outside in the parking lot to discuss personal business. Later I found out we had a snitch in our group. You would be surprised what some officers do to get a good post or a good overtime spot or just to be in a good position with a supervisor. I worked in blocks my whole career (my choice), and I could work anywhere, and I never worried about where I was going to work. I remember when I worked the pen. They kept sending me to the jail to work, so I signed up to be transferred to the jail. They did me a favor, but I'm sure it wasn't their intentions. Some pen officers never worked the jail—hey, whatever works. Some pen officers have never been inside the jail; that's another story entirely, if you know what I mean. I think about my days in the pen, and getting out of there was a blessing in disguise.

Jail politics run deep in the building. You have supervisors who never worked overtime as an officer, but as soon as they were promoted, they worked more overtime than anybody because they picked their posts. How do you respect a person like that, hiding and manipulating the system because of their promotion and current position? As a correctional officer, the incarcerated persons are not the problem. It's a person who has been afraid of the jail environment their whole career, now making decisions based on their position and lack of block experience or knowledge. That person makes the building dangerous, not the incarcerated persons. I'm still wondering how that is allowed? No experience but put in an experienced position. Hopefully, by now, you can see all the drama the officer has to deal with compared to what an incarcerated person has to deal with; and the more I think about it, the officers have it worse. It's not even close the more that I think about it.

As I reminisce about the jail and the penitentiary when I first started, it was off the hook (out of control). If it wasn't for certain officers, the Department of Corrections would have had more riots in the '80s. A lot of those officers no longer work there, but they made a big difference just by being in the building. I won't say their names and bring them unwanted attention, but without you guys back then, that place would have gone under.

During my career, a few officers were taken hostage and locked in cells and locked on the tier of the block. That had to be a traumatic experience for all the officers involved because no guarantees were coming out that situation like you went into it. All it would take is for one of those incarcerated persons to be a little off mentally, and the situation could have gone all the way left. The incarcerated persons had knives, and you could just imagine what was going through the minds of those officers who were taken hostage. That is definitely not a good feeling, and how do you get over something like that mentally? How could you ever feel comfortable in that jail environment again? The average person thinks correctional officers have it made in jail. We go home every night and get paid pretty well. But the reality is, some of us don't make it home every night, unfortunately.

At any given time, the whole jail can go left. Incarcerated persons outnumber the officers on every block you work on, so only a fool would get totally comfortable in that environment. The odds of an officer getting hurt are very high, but you still have officers who think their job is a joke.

You never really know who you are working with until a problem arises, and sometimes the problem could be your partner. I mean, there is a learning curve for everybody. Nobody gets it on the first try; everybody makes mistakes no matter what position you hold in jail. But the key is to do something, and attempting to do something is better than just not doing anything.

The difference in jail, as opposed to the streets, is that as an officer, you have a split second to make a decision and hope it's the right one. On the streets, you have a little more time to think, not too long depending on what's going down, but you do get more time to think about your next move. I know it sounds like jail is a total gloom fest, but we had a few laughs at times. I remember before our shift started in the pen, we used to crack jokes on each other or whoever was around to start our day off on a good note. However, some officers couldn't take a joke and formed a committee, and went to the warden's office to make a complaint. Without any type of investigation, the warden took our names and told our shift captain he was moving us to another building. Our captain vouched for us, and we were not sent out of the building. For the record, I don't think any of us were trying to be malicious; it was just a total misunderstanding because we all got along for the most part. And most of us retired as friends.

I'm going to be honest, without a sense of humor, your career is going to feel like it's going to take one hundred years instead of twenty-five. Even the incarcerated persons understand you have to laugh sometimes, even at the absurdity of how things unravel. It's amazing how after only a few years, the effects of the jail are noticeable on both officers and incarcerated persons. The concrete floors are a killer on your back, knees, legs, hips, feet, and ankles. After being exposed to that floor, one or a few of these are going to be an issue, whether you are an officer or an incarcerated person. They should explore getting maybe a type of shoe or sneaker made to absorb some of the shock that presently your body parts currently absorb walking on that concrete floor.

I wonder if studies have been done to show the effects of one's body walking on concrete floors for an extended amount of time. I'm sure it will not be favorable to the person exposed to this dilemma. Just imagine if the NBA used concrete courts; how long a basketball player's career would be, maybe five years at the most. They have a floor that gives a bit, and the injury count is still up there. So you can imagine, if they use the same floor we use, they would get the same results, probably in a quicker time because of their approach of jumping and running on that substance. It's a subject I hope one day somebody looks into because you can't continue to witness the effects of this concrete floor on corrections officers' bodies and not do anything about it.

If they took a poll, you would be surprised how many officers are affected by this. Those steel gates are nothing to play with. Imagine opening and closing a steel gate weighing about 250 pounds or more every day. What effect would that have on your arm joints over a twenty-year period? That's interesting, but I'm sure it will be years or decades before we get answers to these questions. If I could suggest one thing to the officers, it would be to document all your injuries throughout your career and keep a diary so if the need arises, you can refer back to it. Keep your paperwork tight; you never know when you might need it. Okay, I'm sure you get the picture.

Once you're working as a corrections officer, you have to decide almost immediately whether you want to be a leader or a follower. Most people who pick followers run into some problems along the way because in jail, the followers are usually the equivalent of the blind leading the blind. If you're not sure about something, ask someone. We had an officer who convinced a rookie officer to put on an infectious disease suit to escort an incarcerated person to the clinic. Now, this suit is bright white and is mainly used by incarcerated persons to clean up blood or other body fluids off the floor or on the walls. Anyway, this rookie officer was walking through the building, and people are laughing their heads off. Even the incarcerated person the officer is escorting is looking at the officer like, *Are you OK?* and laughing to themselves. Supervisors even witnessed this officer walking around the building with this bright white suit on and said nothing. It was kind of funny, but it could have been avoided if the rookie officer just asked somebody else about wearing that white suit. Again, my motto is "Trust no one." If you're not sure about something, ask somebody else. Don't let anybody clown you like that because the jail never forgets a laugh, especially like that. There's no such thing as knowing it all, and yeah, the people who act like they have all the answers never actually listen to the questions.

We had another rookie officer who allowed an incarcerated person to give him a haircut. He was supposed to be watching the incarcerated persons and getting his haircut. Imagine if an incarcerated person gets assaulted on his block while he is getting the haircut. Plus, he has his back to the incarcerated persons, and they have razors, scissors, and other sharp instruments they can use, unbelievable. How could a rookie think that it's OK to get a haircut from an incarcerated person? Like I said, we all make mistakes, but that's something different. I know when you first start the job, there is a feeling-out process; but at some point, your common sense and street smarts have to kick in, and you'll be fine. And most rookies will be alright anyway,. You always have a few that just don't get it. I think every year I worked for the Department of Corrections, several people were fired for a number of different situations and circumstances. It appears to be a lot stricter now because we had people you wouldn't believe if you didn't see it with your own eyes or hear it with your own ears.

I was very fortunate when I started working in the pen. My trustee was a person I knew from the streets, Lenny Barnes (I got his permission to use his name). He was very helpful in helping me learn the routine and the pen. I didn't know how to run a block when I started. Lenny was always a good dude, and he didn't have any problems in the pen with anybody. I say that because the pen was overcrowded at the time, and it seemed like everybody had a problem with everybody. It was total mass confusion in the blocks, and Lenny gave me a heads up on the do's and don'ts. I trusted Lenny probably more than some of my coworkers because he was always the same, never changed up like some people are known to do. Lenny Barnes was a cool brother; we still keep in touch. Most of the officers respected Lenny Barnes, and he had no problems through-out the buildings.

Things always go a lot smoother when you know what you're supposed to be doing. You meet a lot of interest-ing people in jail, hear a lot, see a lot. Jail changes you after a while. It gives a gradual change, not overnight; but over the course of your career, you will notice a change in your personality. Sometimes it's good, sometimes it's bad, but it's still a change. My change, I think, has been posi-tive. Although I have more compassion for people, I have a low tolerance for bullcrap. I can hear the tone in a person's voice and the words they use and know immediately how I'm going to deal with the situation. I don't know if it's a gift or a curse. I look back on my career and think about the officers who were killed outside of the job and the ones who had to kill to defend themselves.

The streets are just as dangerous for us as it is for anybody else. But the goal is to make it back home to your family by any means necessary. It's unfortunate, but this is the society we live in. That's why it's not worth arguing with anybody anymore. Let it go; it's not worth the court appearances and the paperwork. However, if my family is threatened, that changes everything. Overall, I try to avoid trouble if I can because life is too short to spend any more of my time behind bars. Most of us already did twenty-five years. Don't you think that's enough? It's not easy, but we have to protect ourselves now or face the consequences. Sometimes it feels like the corrections officer is the scapegoat of Corrections when something goes wrong; just blame it on the officer. "That should be an easy sell"—it almost feels like the motto that the administration lives by. It's like the officers and the incarcerated persons are portrayed as the villains in the Department of Corrections, but that's hardly the case. If the officers and the incarcerated persons didn't mutually respect one another, no system outside of that would be effective.

I said this before: communication skills are a must. There is a certain way people with respect communicate with each other. I don't know any adult who is OK with somebody talking down to them and yelling because, personally, I give you the same energy you give, no matter what your job title is. I was an employee; I'm not your child. I used to see grown men and women act like kids when certain supervisors came around. I stayed away from those officers. I didn't want anybody to confuse me with being one of them. To me, respect is never negotiable; I can't live without it. Some people pick and choose whom they give respect to. I respect everyone until they give me a reason not to.

I remember when I first started the job, an officer I thought I knew said he was sending down two incarcerated persons to get a mattress. They came to my gate, and I gave them the mattress. Five minutes later, a sergeant called me and asked me what these two incarcerated persons were doing with a mattress. I said, "Officer Blue [not his real name] told me to send it." The sergeant told the officer what I said, and I could hear his response: "Evans is lying." The sergeant hung up the phone. I called the desk and told them I needed a break. They sent me an officer for a break, and I went straight to the officer's post. He opened the gate and said, "Don't worry about it." I told him, "You better find somebody else to play with. If you ever try something like that again, we both are going to lose our jobs." We never ever spoke again after that, and it was best we didn't.

After that incident, I really never trusted anybody. As I worked there, I saw how officers used to pull pranks on one another, but I wasn't with it. My experience has shown me that once in a while, you come across an incarcerated person or two who doesn't want to follow the rules. However, most of the nonsense you have to deal with comes from the officers or administration. The incarcerated persons know which officers are fair, and they can work with them. They also know the officers with whom they just can't vibe. It happens; no officer gets along with everybody, and no incarcerated person gets along with everybody. That's life;

that's how it is sometimes. But it's in everybody's best interest when things go smooth. It sets a pleasant tone throughout the block, and most of the time, it mellows out the whole block when things go smooth. Maintaining your professionalism, especially when everything around you is just the opposite, is a job within itself. Sometimes officers are most certainly tested—testing the officers' patience and their good work ethic. I mean, you're going to run into incarcerated persons who are going to push you to the edge, but you have to remember you have too much to lose for you to lose focus. If you lose focus, no matter the outcome, the incarcerated person wins by default. So keep your eyes on the prize, which is retirement.

Twenty-five years seems like a long time, but looking back, it's almost like a blur. I remember some things, but some things I don't. After twenty-five years, a lot has happened, but my main emphasis is showing the similarities between the officer and the incarcerated person. It's not an exact comparison, but close enough to garner attention and start the conversation. I watched a documentary recently about coal miners: their working conditions, life expectancy, pay, and health benefits. As I watched it, I realized that they are faced with most of the same dilemmas that we are faced with. The life expectancy of a coal miner is thirty-nine while the life expectancy of a corrections officer is fifty-eight. Working in a coal mine is dangerous, just like working in a jail. Coal miners have to deal with toxic gases, the threat of being crushed, or drowning. However, the pay is pretty good, but every day you go to work, it could be your last. The description sounds just like the correction officer's environment. There are definitely toxic people in jail. Coming home every day is not guaranteed for the officer; however, the pay is good, and overtime helps. These two jobs resemble each other a lot.

I was watching that documentary and couldn't help but notice its similarities to corrections. In spite of all the dangers and the low life expectancy rate for both professions, I'm sure if either side had to answer the question, "Why gamble with your life?" most would say, "Because it takes care of my family." It's sad on so many levels. So many lives have been lost, and we continue to lose people because they're trying to feed thcir families. In corrections, it sometimes looks like a suicide mission because most of us don't make it out. More should be done to monitor the officers' mental and physical health because a lot of concerns don't make sense. A person would be shocked how certain simple things are not monitored, and the major things get totally ignored.

If a person is not active outside of work, it could be a very unhealthy decision moving forward for them. I hope officers become more proactive with their health; it's beyond important. The reality of the jail is, both the officer and the incarcerated persons are doing time, and through the years, it takes a toll on an officer mentally and physically. After your career is over and you can walk out of that building on your own, count your blessings because those twenty-five years are like running a marathon; and just like a marathon, everybody who starts doesn't finish. When you see the number of people who don't finish, it just goes to show what an honor and a blessing it is to cross the finish line into the threshold of retirement. It's the ultimate blessing of a corrections officer.

The incarcerated person's goal is similar to ours. They want to get out of jail alive. It's their goal to walk out of that jail when their time is up. Nobody wants to die in jail or die while working for the jail. Everybody wants to get out alive, which is understandable. That's what we all are working toward: the day we don't have to hear that jail noise anymore.

The experience of going into the jail is almost identical for the officer and the incarcerated person. Before the officer is hired, he is fingerprinted, and his picture is taken. Before an incarcerated person comes to jail, he is fingerprinted, and his picture is taken. Before the incarcerated person enters the blocks, he is given clothes to wear. Before an officer enters the jail, he is given clothes to wear. The incarcerated person is given rules and regulations of what's expected of them. The officer is given SOPs (standing operations procedures,) which are the rules and regulations of what's expected of them. The incarcerated person is told what he can wear on his feet. The officer is told what he can wear on their feet. The incarcerated person is told when to eat. The officer is told when they can go to eat. Neither the officer nor the incarcerated person can do exactly what they want to do; both need the permission of the Department of Corrections to do anything. Not too much difference, really.

I remember when we entered the academy, we had to drag a fifty-pound bag up a flight of stairs and bring it back down. There was this guy who looked like he spent a lot of time in the gym, and he attempted to drag the bag, and he was falling all over the place. I thought he was playing around, but he wasn't; he had no balance. He couldn't run a straight line. After a couple of minutes of failed attempts, he was stopped and sent home. Looking at him, you never would have thought he would fail that part of the academy. We lost a lot of officers in the academy, and I don't feel it was anything difficult. I think some people just had some physical issues that prohibited them from getting the job.

Our first day in the building, we lined up in front of the pen, and an officer showed up looking like a hockey player—knee pads, elbow pads, mouthpiece, and a football helmet. The sergeant took one look at him and said, "Take all that equipment off, and don't ever let me see you wear it again." We all got a good laugh, and it broke the ice and made most of us more comfortable going into the building. I will never forget that day, and to think twenty-five years is over just like that. After your career is over and you retire, it's almost like a rude awakening of what just happened. You ask yourself, How did I stay in that environment as long as I did, and what effect will it have on my life going forward? The job wreaks havoc on your health and your family if you're not careful. I don't have the exact numbers, but the amount of officers who don't make it to retirement is mind-boggling. Sometimes you have to ask yourself how many officers have to get hurt before the Department of Corrections does something to correct the problem or if the problem can be corrected.

If every year at least five officers get severely hurt at the same location in the jail, what do you think? That is a problem going forward. Twenty-five years is a long time to be in one place, especially when that place is toxic, dangerous, and mentally unhealthy. All the time I hear officers who have retired talking about needing to detox themselves from that jail environment, myself included. It's inevitable for everybody who has spent an extended time in jail to detox themselves when they get out; it's practically synonymous with retirement. Growing up, if somebody would have told me that I was going to work in a jail for twenty-five years, I would have said, "You sound crazy." Coming up in life, jail is a place you try to avoid at all costs. I was raised to believe it's next to the last place you want to be, next to dead. Jail was a very negative subject that we hardly talked about, but most people painted a negative picture of jail when they would talk about it. However, many years later, I find myself working for the Department of Corrections.

In my twenty-five years, the only time I have ever thought we were headed down a dangerous slope was when the administration decided to classify the jail as a smoke-free zone, meaning cigarettes were no longer allowed in jail. Cigarettes were incarcerated persons' currency at the time; almost every part of their life in jail was funded by cigarettes. They would use cigarettes to have their clothes washed by other incarcerated persons on the block, and cigarettes were traded among them for food. Like I said, cigarettes were a very big part of incarcerated persons' culture, and to ban cigarettes, I thought we were in for a disaster on the day the ban would start.

Officers were calling in sick to avoid that day because they just knew that it was going to be a dangerous day when the ban started. I remember it was a little extra quiet, which usually means the calm before the storm, but to my surprise, nothing happened that day that I know of. Not one incident did I observe due to the banning of cigarettes. It turned out to be one of the best decisions made in my career. It afforded officers and incarcerated persons clean air. I remember the blocks used to be smoke-filled where you could hardly breathe, but since the ban on cigarettes, clean air was long overdue. Looking back, that was a great decision.

Another thing that was a major problem when I started was the boomboxes with the D batteries. Those were also banned during my career, and for good reason. The noise level was insane, and plus, the D batteries in a sock were a serious weapon. I knew a few incarcerated person who lost an eye from getting hit in the face with a sock full of D batteries. So banning the boomboxes killed two birds with one stone. And now you can hear the announcements over the intercom. The quality of life got better by the day. They substituted the boomboxes for Walkmans. Most young people don't even know what a Walkman is and how rapidly technology is changing.

OK, since administration was on a roll with banning a lot of the incarcerated persons' pastime recreational devices, they decided that they would also ban the free weights—no more weight lifting. Imagine a jail that no longer allows weight lifting. I always thought that someone would use the weight bar as a weapon if a fight broke out in the yard, but that never happened because we had, back then, a good rec officer and an incarcerated-person rec crew, and the respect was there. I thought banning the weights was pushing it, asking for a problem, but just like every other ban, nobody made any noise, and the weights were removed from the jail and the pen forever. True story.

Incarcerated-person visits are probably the best thing for incarcerated persons, next to going home. Most incarcerated persons appear more comfortable and in better spirits when they are around their loved ones. It gives them approximately thirty minutes of a familiar vibe and inter-action that they are used to. The visiting room is an area where you have to be paying close attention because that is probably the primary place where contraband is passed to the incarcerated person. I remember when I started, incar-cerated persons and visitors would try to switch sneak-ers, and baby's diapers would be used to conceal drugs or other contraband. Even something as simple as a note on a piece of paper could be made out of a certain substance. In the visiting room, you have to be alert, no less than effective, because if they catch you sleeping or not alert, they're going to attempt something. It happens, and you can't ever say one person is more suspicious than the other, period, because—you would be surprised—in jail, nobody gets a pass.

I remember if an incarcerated person wanted to go see the doctor, they had to fill out a sick call slip. But they would get upset when I handed them the slip of paper with three questions on it: (1) name, (2) location, (3) illness, and most refused to fill it out. Then one day, an incarcer-ated person explained to me that most of these guys can't read and write, which makes sense. So I started filling it out for them because all they had to do is tell me their name. Problem solved. But something like that could have resulted in a problem for real if you don't know what the real problem is, which brings me to repeating myself: the incarcerated person and the officers have to work together. There is no way around it, especially if you're striving for peace in the block and want your day to go smoothly. The lack of education and incarceration are closely related.

I always told myself when I was working, "It's not brain surgery," and the officers who act like it's brain surgery, I try to avoid them. Let me be honest: being in jail sucks, whether you're an officer or an incarcerated person. There is nothing like having your freedom to go about your business and do what you want to do. But for us officers, bills have to be paid, and for incarcerated persons, their debt to society has to be paid. But jail, especially sucks during the holidays, more specifically Christmas. More suicides happen with officers and incarcerated persons around that time of year than any other time of year. Depression is real; nothing is worse than being in jail, no matter if you're an officer or an incarcerated person locked up, and your world on the outside is falling apart.

All across this country, in probably every jail you can think of, we lose officers and incarcerated persons in record numbers to depression and suicides. It's a serious problem that officers unfortunately have front-row seats to. I know I touched on this subject earlier in the book, but enough can never be said to try and save lives. God bless the families that have personally dealt with this situation; may prayers come your way continuously. In my twenty-five years as a corrections officer, I have seen more deaths than any other period of my life, and it never gets any easier. Sometimes it's an incarcerated person who just went home or an officer you just worked with the other day. It's something you will never get used to.

Every time I turn on the news on TV and hear about a shooting in my old hometown Mount Vernon, it's beyond

sad that another life is lost over some foolishness or an inno-
cent bystander. It has to stop; something has to be done.
However, I'm encouraged because the mayor, Shawyn
Patterson-Howard, is doing a great job.

I also would like to know why corrections officers die
at such an accelerated rate. Officers get sick, and you will
never see them again, or we attend their funerals. What is it
about the Department of Corrections that seems to trigger
heart attacks and strokes and compels officers to commit
suicide? Nothing is more important than saving and pre-
serving life. We have to do better as a society. Remember,
the life expectancy of a corrections officer is fifty-eight years
old or five years beyond retirement, so anything over that,
you are living on borrowed time, according to research. I
know nobody lives forever. I get that. My own father died
in March 2022 at the age of ninety-four. He was a retired
construction worker, and he was married to my mother
for sixty-six years. Had my father only been in my life for
a short period of time or not at all, I would have been a
totally different person. My father was my example of what
a man is supposed to be. He raised us to have confidence,
respect, work hard, and choose family first. Growing up,
I idolized my father, my uncles, and a few of my friends'
fathers. I took a little from each, and that's who I am today,
thank God.

I can't write this book without giving our union a
shout-out. I mentioned the union earlier, but I want to be
specific. I want to thank everybody who has worked in our
union throughout my career to the present. That's a hard
job, but you guys get it done. A lot of officers would get

railroaded if it wasn't for the union. Thanks for your hard work, and you will always have my support.

I also have to share something I felt was kind of bizarre. I think it was around 2015 or 2016. The union president debate was getting ready to start. I went to observe and just to see a few people I had not seen in a while. The union sent a rookie in my direction and said I couldn't attend the debate. At first, I started to say something, but I chose to remain professional and left without incident. I had lost all respect for everybody in the union at that point. That's how you treat your retired officers? I support the people who are there now. They seem more competent and professional, and from what I'm hearing, they are doing a great job. God bless. Karma is something else: everybody who was involved with denying me entry into the debate, look at them now. You can't make this up. Do they still believe in the system now? Good luck with that. I apologize to my readers, but I had to get that off my chest. Throughout the writing of this book, I'm writing about my experience and my perceptions of things I have observed in my career.

As I pointed out earlier, no two people have the exact same experience in jail, so it's fully acceptable that someone who worked in the jail would have a different experience than mine. The key word is *mine*. I truly believe nothing in jail is really personal. It's a system that isn't perfect, but it deals with everybody in that building almost in the same way. It depends on how you are and which way jail will respond to you. I had officers who I thought I knew, but when they were under a little pressure, they folded like a lawn chair. All I wanted was for them to tell the truth, and they started auditioning for *Rain Man*. Thank God for the warden for bringing out the truth. I will never forget that. When somebody really shows you who they are, believe them. People talk the talk but don't walk the walk. You will be surprised who will change up on you without a warning. It happens so frequently you begin to expect it. In jail, you can never predict the outcome.

I heard a male incarcerated person was assaulting a male officer, and a female officer pulled the male incarcerated person off the officer and restrained him until the team showed up. That happens a lot, to tell you the truth. I never actually saw it happen, but that's not the first time I heard a female officer had to save a male officer from an incarcerated person. I guess the world is changing. I'm going to leave that right there. I think I said in the first chapter the job is not for everybody. Some people catch on quick, and for some people, it takes a while. But if you don't quit or get fired, eventually you will get it. I'm sure you just have to have patience sometimes and hopefully a good training officer.

At that point, I knew I couldn't trust anybody on that job. It was worse for some officers, but I won't even get into that. I'm sure they got a few incarcerated persons in trouble. Someone asked me how the morale in jail is. I said, "I don't know about now, but when I was there, morale was kind of low because of favoritism, nepotism, preferential treatment—you name it. It kills the morale when you see a person have three days on the job and have it better than the officer who has five years but is not related to someone at the so-called top. What's really hard to swallow is that they have only a week on the job but actually try to tell you how to do a job you've been doing for over twenty-five years. It would be funny if it wasn't so pathetic, but most people keep it moving because complaining only falls on deaf ears. Nobody cares. Plus, you don't want to get the label of always complaining about something. I don't know what's worse, a know-it-all a or complainer—the jury is still out on that one.

Working in corrections takes a little luck, a lot of street smarts and common sense, and a prayer. Anything can happen at any time, and you can never predict what kind of day you're about to have or how it's going to turn out. We have all seen officers who couldn't run their blocks if they were paying the incarcerated person to do the right thing, but when they miraculously get promoted, all of a sudden they become know-it-alls with a bunch of made-up stories to tell at payback day. It just downright insults your intelligence. I never played make-believe when I was growing up, so as an adult, it's definitely a hard pill to swallow watching and listening to a bunch of people make up stuff that never happened, and you know their history in the blocks. It's misleading to some and downright disrespectful to those who actually do the job without the Disney intro.

OK, let me keep it positive. Like I said earlier, there are some things I don't miss. Getting back on track. Early on in my career in the pen, different churches would come into the pen and worship with the incarcerated persons, and sometimes the message would be so powerful that the officers and the incarcerated persons would benefit from the experience. I remember a few times I felt like I had been to church over the years. They had some very good speakers or an ex-incarcerated person who got himself together and now has an inspiring story and testimony to tell. We all are on this earth for a purpose, and only God knows what that purpose is. We are all on a journey, and nobody knows what our destiny is. All I can say is enjoy the ride and trust nobody because in jail, it's just like the streets: a second chance is not guaranteed, so step wisely. Working with the wrong person, you could probably find yourself doing more time than the incarcerated person you're watching because, let's face it, some officers have a different agenda. You could be trying to do the job, but they're trying to get validation from the incarcerated person. At times, it looks like high school all over again.

When the system is flawed, everybody under the flawed umbrella gets wet. It doesn't exclude the officer or the incarcerated person. The officer and incarcerated person have to work together for the blocks to maintain a civilized society. As an officer, you have to get your trustee and most of the incarcerated persons to buy into your system of running your block in peace and hopefully uneventful. In jail, the average person who hasn't seen the inside of a jail thinks the only person who would suffer from the stressed-out environment is the incarcerated persons. However, some officers are also candidates for stress. Actually, for anybody exposed to a long-term jail environment, stress is in their future. Nobody who works there is immune. Depression, strokes, and heart attacks are becoming synonymous with corrections officers.

The big picture is that it's not a healthy environment for anybody, mentally or physically. Numbers don't lie. In some jails all across this country, every day an officer is being injured, and his or her career could be over. Back in the old days, corrections officers used what is called a turn-key. It could open the cell, and it was capable of shooting one round in case there was a problem. Today the officer doesn't carry anything on their person to assist them with a problem except a body alarm, and even then, it takes a few minutes for your help to arrive. Anybody can tell you it doesn't take but a split second for you to become severely injured on any given day or moment in jail.

Working in a jail comes with a lot of responsibility. One wrong move and one bad decision can cause a catastrophe. You almost have to think three steps ahead so you don't fall one step behind. During my career, there were always a few people you could talk to who would give you good advice. Most of those guys, if not all of them, have since retired. You respected their knowledge on things; and some, if they didn't have the answer, they would get it. I think most jails are like that, a few guys who are walking reference books to the Department of Corrections. I don't know how it is now, but I'm sure there are some up-and-coming officers, hopefully with a wealth of information, ready to help a fellow officer in need.

To be honest, however, during my last couple of years there, I didn't see the camaraderie among officers that I was used to when I started. Unfortunately, it seems we are living in the *me* era, not the *we* era. Everybody for themselves. You even see the mentality in sports. Passing the ball is a lost art form; nobody really does it anymore. Quarterbacks now have more yards than some running backs. Running a jail successfully is definitely a team sport. Everybody has to be on the same page, working together; otherwise, anything outside of that is wasted effort, which is going to get disastrous results when it comes to operating a jail.

I know a lot of procedures have changed. Are they better or worse? That can be debated, but the changes have reduced the liability to the jail, and now it appears the officer is on the hook when problems arise. Did they act or respond in description of their duties? You see it all the time on the news, the newspaper, on the internet—officers getting in trouble over the way they did their job, with excessive force or bodily harm. Legal liability is a reality a lot of jails are implementing; jail employees may be legally liable for their actions.

Going forward, the law enforcement liability at some point would be solely on the employee, which I'm sure will change the dynamics of the job. When you think about it, for officers who quit the job, got fired, or didn't make it past the academy, maybe that was some form of divine intervention. They avoided being locked up and exposing their minds and body to all the chaos in the jail that you have to deal with on a daily basis. Most officers come into the building respectfully obeying all the rules and regulations, but as time goes by, you start seeing the real character of some of the people you work with, and it makes it very difficult to respect their vision or leadership. Since I have been retired, I have seen at least three supervisors, one in particular who was always involved in something, on the news and the newspaper, and it wasn't because they were receiving some type of award for citizen of the year. You see that it's a black eye on corrections. We already have a negative image to most for a lot of different reasons. Nevertheless, when these horrific stories hit the media, it's a bad day for the Department of Corrections as a whole. Like I wrote, I put this book together to show officers and incarcerated persons similarities, but I also feel compelled to elaborate on a few things I found newsworthy while I was there.

The job is beyond interesting. Something is always happening, whether it be the officer or the incarcerated person, and sometimes both are involved. I know you have read those stories online or seen them on the news or in the newspaper. That's why you have to always be thinking and alert because you don't want to get involved in anything that's going to get you time in jail if you're an officer, and more time in jail if you're an incarcerated person. I bet there are a lot of interesting statistics associated with running a jail, and I would guess that the numbers for the officers and the incarcerated persons are almost identical. But aside from those numbers, these are real people these things are happening to—officers and incarcerated persons. They are faced with horrible conditions on a daily basis.

Officers spend their whole careers trying to convince incarcerated people in jail that it is not that bad, and the administration tries to convince the officers working in jail that it is not that bad. However, over time, both the officer and the incarcerated person have a multitude of issues related to being exposed to a jail for long periods. It's a life sentence no matter how you look at it. And it not only affects the individual who is behind those walls, but the families of those individuals as well. Jail has a more far-reaching effect on society than most could imagine. It's most definitely something to think about.

Looking back, we lost a lot of good human beings for a number of different reasons, and we will continue to watch our brothers and sisters prematurely perish until something is done to eradicate the stress so officers are not prone to depression, heart attacks, strokes, and not compelled to overindulge in alcohol consumption and drug use. And hopefully, things can start turning around because every year we lose a lot of officers and incarcerated persons from the present association of jail culture. In closing, I hope those who read this book found it informative, entertaining at times, and interesting. Thanks for reading it; that's all I ask. God bless and take care.

AFTERWORD

As a corrections officer, jail can make or break a person, considering their life experience. Some officers get the job and have no idea what they're about to be exposed to. That's why so many officers don't make it because they get the job thinking they are going to walk around the jail with some type of protection, and that's totally not the case. Most of the time, you can't rely on anything but yourself and common sense because help is not immediate; it takes a few minutes, so those few minutes can be the deciding factor for an officer, whether you're going to sustain an injury or not. Minutes in jail can feel like an hour if you need immediate help in this situation on your block or the rec yard. Three minutes could feel like forever. Just looking back over my career, there are so many traps you can fall into as an officer if you're not on your A game. I can't stress it enough: you have to constantly be alert, or you're going to find yourself in a bunch of nonsense.

I have seen so many officers, male and female, unfortunately, get involved in situations that cost them their jobs and some of them their freedom. I'm sure when they first got the job, they had the best of intentions, but not everybody has the same life experience. Being from Mount

Vernon, you grow up in a boot camp for life environment. You're raised around some of the best that ever did it, so you recognize real and you know the fake from a mile away. Mount Vernon had a lot of street legends, too many to name, and some are no longer with us, but may they rest in peace. I learned a lot from them. A lot has changed; now it's not the same in those streets. Everybody in the streets is trying to take shortcuts, and their lives are being cut short. The senseless killings have to stop. Kids should feel safe when they go out in their communities. Let's work on that. Anything is possible with faith.

The Department of Corrections overall is a good job. You have a lot of hardworking people doing a job with no weapons. I can't say this enough: it's more mental than physical. Only the mentally strong people survive in the jail environment. Everybody's goal is almost the same: to get through the day and take care of their families. Nothing is more important than that. It's, without question, a hard job mentally, but you get through it for the greater good. I can't help but think of all the people we lost in my twenty-five-year career and beyond. My prayers are with their families, and may their loved ones continue to rest in eternal paradise. It's a hard job, but somebody has to do it.

The goal of writing this book was to show how the jail environment affects the officers and the incarcerated person in a similar way. Also, I inserted where I saw fit different situations and circumstances officers and incarcerated persons find themselves, and again, this is my perspective on jail. I'm not looking for anybody to agree with me or disagree with me because this is how I saw things in my twenty-five years of being in the jail environment. It's been real. I met a lot of good people in my years there, and I pray all is well with them and their families.

We had a small circle because we didn't include any squares. We laughed and joked a lot, and when it was time to be serious, that wasn't a problem. Nothing is perfect; there is always room for improvement. However, there is a saying, "If it's not broken, don't fix it." Translation: if it's working, leave it alone. Like I said before, I keep in touch with mostly guys I was in the academy with and someone who was not in the academy with me. The common denominator with everyone is that they are glad to be out of that place. I even keep in touch with some other incarcerated persons who were cool with me, like Lenny Barnes on the inside. We lost a lot of them to the streets under some of the same circumstances we lost officers. Like it or not, we are all connected in some form or fashion for life because we all have similar experiences and reactions from the exposure to the jail environment. But the million-dollar question is, Where do we go from here? Only God knows. Thanks for taking this journey with me. Hope you enjoyed the book. Take care. Peace.

I'd like to thank everyone who read this book and got something out of it. The main purpose of this book was to show that nobody has it that good in jail, not the officers nor the incarcerated persons. They both are just trying to make the best out of that situation. For the most part, it all works out in the long run. I guess it's something about being in jail that makes a person more reasonable. They're up for discussion where if these same individuals were in the streets, I'm sure some things would have been handled differently. So thank God for jail in respect to those types of situations that, when presented on the streets, result in the loss of life.

In the hood, guns are part of the problem, not part of the solution. A disagreement among two people should never result in a loss of life; it's never that serious. No person should ever be able to get you all up in your feelings because if they control your emotions, they control you. Your ego will always be a threat to your peace of mind, so if I had to pick one, *peace of mind* wins every time. Stay focused, brothers and sisters, and let us stop dying of street rage so we can start thinking about old age because all this violence has got to stop! Let's start saving lives. We have to start doing better because we definitely know better. There is no excuse going forward.

BONUS PAGE

I know you thought the book was over, but I have a lot to say on this subject. Working in a jail for over twenty-five years, I have seen a lot. I have seen officers get chased off blocks, and I have seen incarcerated persons get chased off blocks. Nothing is sacred in jail; anything can happen to anybody. Nobody is immune from the violence, the disrespect, and the dysfunction that the jail sometimes breeds. However, the jail cannot operate without respect being distributed on *both sides*—it's never a one-way street. It can be frustrating, humiliating, and even devastating for some. However the vibe is at the time, the climate of the environment, or even the calmness we may experience from time to time, just remember this piece of information that will forever be a fact: no matter what's going on at the time, it's still JAIL.

Waulee Evans knows it's impossible to write his whole entire career in one book. However, he tried to expound on the highlights and incidents that he can recall during his twenty-five years in the department of corrections. Waulee attempted to show you through this book that inmates and officers experience almost identical anxiety and stress, both mentally and physically, from their exposure from the department of corrections. No two days are exactly alike, and no two people in jail have the exact same experience. However, the end results on the officers and the inmates are too similar to ignore.

This book is an attempt to get officers to think more seriously about the department of corrections and their physical and mental health.

2 Timothy 1:7 "For God gave us a spirit not of fear but of power and love and self-control." God bless.

www.ingramcontent.com/pod-product-compliance
Lightning Source LLC
Chambersburg PA
CBHW032017090426
42741CB00006B/637